The Mindful Education
WORKBOOK

ALSO BY DANIEL J. RECHTSCHAFFEN

The Way of Mindful Education:
Cultivating Well-Being in Teachers and Students

NORTON BOOKS IN EDUCATION

The Mindful
Education
WORKBOOK

Lessons for Teaching
Mindfulness to Students

DANIEL J. RECHTSCHAFFEN

W.W. NORTON & COMPANY

Independent Publishers Since 1923

New York / London

Interior illustrations by Micah Cohen, micahcohen.net; micahcreek@gmail.com

For information about permission to reproduce selections from this book, write to Permissions, W. W. Norton & Company, Inc., 500 Fifth Avenue, New York, NY 10110

For information about special discounts for bulk purchases, please contact W. W. Norton Special Sales at specialsales@wwnorton.com or 800-233-4830

Manufacturing by Maple Press
Book design by Carole Desnoes
Production manager: Christine Critelli

Library of Congress Cataloging-in-Publication Data

Names:
Rechtschaffen, Daniel J., author.
Title: The mindful education workbook :
lessons for teaching mindfulness to
   students / Daniel
Rechtschaffen.
Description: First edition. | New York :
W.W. Norton &
Company, [2016] |
   Series: Norton books in education | Includes
bibliographical references
   and index.
Identifiers: LCCN 2015046822 |
ISBN 9780393710465 (pbk.)
Subjects: LCSH: Attention. | Mindfulness
(Psychology) | Educational
   psychology. | Mindfulness-based cognitive
therapy.
Classification: LCC LB1065 .R3867 2016 | DDC 371.102—dc23 LC
record available at http://lccn.loc.gov/2015046822

W. W. Norton & Company, Inc.
500 Fifth Avenue, New York, N.Y. 10110
www.wwnorton.com

W. W. Norton & Company Ltd.
Castle House, 75/76 Wells Street, London W1T 3QT

1 2 3 4 5 6 7 8 9 0

For Taylor.
My wife, my friend,
my teacher, my compañera.

Contents

Acknowledgments

Deepest gratitude goes to my students, who have taught me the art of playing mindfulness. So many of the lessons in this book were inspired or directly taught to me by students and teachers who took these teachings and evolved them in ways I never would have imagined.

I am indebted to the schools and organizations that have given me a home to implement the teachings in this book. I particularly want to thank the Marin Preparatory School, the SEEDS of Awareness community, Mindful Schools, as well as all the educators who have taken the learning journeys with me through the Mindful Education Institute and Mindful Education workshops.

To Linda Lantieri for her mentorship. I have never met someone as whole heartedly committed to the inner lives of kids. To Daniel Siegel for his shining mind and heart and for playing a key role in helping me publish my books. To Susan Kaiser-Greenland, who has been a guiding light for me in her profound creativity and the way she embodies mindfulness in her teaching. To Jamie Zimmerman—we carry the legacy of your beautiful heart and visionary work with us. There are so many in the mindful education community I have the honor of calling my friends and colleagues. Here are just a few I want to name because of how much I have learned from them and how deeply I respect the work they are doing: Jennifer Cohen Harper, Iamani Carrey-Simms, Melody Baker, Gina Biegal, Ali Smith, Atman Smith, Andy Garcia, Tish Jennings, Michael Craft, Meena Srinivasan, Theo Koffler, Laurie Grossman, Richard Shankman, Megan Cowan, Chris McKenna, Vinny Ferraro, Shauna Shapiro, Richard Burnett, Chris Cullen, Sam Himelstein, Jessica Morey, Marylin Neagley, Ryan Redman,

Daniella Labra, Amishi Jha, Richie Davidson, Spring Washam, J. G. Larochete, JusTme, B. K. Bose, Morris Ervin, Howard Moody, Rachel Brown, Mim Kohn, Emily Weiner, and Peter Bonnano.

I understand that bringing mindfulness into the education system is a phenomenon only possible because of the forward-thinking minds and diligent work of those who have come before me. My mother, Elizabeth Lesser, and father, Stephan Rechtschaffen, have been foundational in bringing wisdom traditions into the mainstream and offering me a truly mindful upbringing. Having founded and directed the Omega Institute, they gave me the gift of growing up surrounded by luminaries whom I have had the honor of learning from, such as Jon Kabat-Zinn, Daniel Goleman, Thich Nhat Hanh, Joan Halifax, John and Jennifer Welwood, and so many others. I thank all of those whose vision and diligence have validated the benefits of mindfulness and emotional intelligence so that we now can integrate these invaluable practices into schools.

To Benjamin Yarling, Deborah Malmud, and the rest of the remarkable Norton team. The seed of this workbook was planted by your faith in my vision, and the support you have shown through every step has brought these pages to full bloom. Also to Micah Cohen for bringing beauty to these pages with his amazing art.

The Mindful Education

WORKBOOK

GETTING STARTED

The Mindfulness in Education Movement

Schools across the world are turning to mindfulness in the hopes that it will be an antidote for rising stress, emotional dysregulation, and attention deficit. In researching the school systems that have adopted mindfulness, we are learning that students and teachers are happier, more focused, emotionally regulated, and less affected by stress (Zenner et al., 2014). What school would pass up a chance to raise test scores, have fewer playground fights, and cultivate a more peaceful environment?

In South Burlington, Vermont, students begin and end each day with a few mindful minutes, focusing on their breath and building their attention muscles. In Baltimore, Maryland, high schoolers walk into the chill room when they need to cool down from stressful situations, working with impulse control and learning to communicate when there is conflict. In Sun Valley, Idaho students practice compassion in school and then make it real by choosing community service projects in their town, even traveling around the world bringing their empathic commitment. Students from Mexico to Israel to Rwanda are learning mindfulness in creative and inspiring ways.

Apps and online programs have been developed to teach these concepts in a way many find fun and accessible. There are now mindfulness in education programs with videos and recordings where all the teachers need to lead a lesson is press play. Hip-hop artists are putting out albums for kids to teach them to breathe and relax over a funky beat. Artist and mindfulness teacher JustMe has a song called Mindful Life in which the chorus repeats, "I'm showing up every school day, being present without judgment is the new thing."

Mindfulness is not just for kids, of course. Sometimes after our students have learned mindfulness, we may have the beautiful and humbling experience of having them look at us and say, "You look stressed. Do you need to take a mindful moment to relax?" There are now many programs and school initiatives that promote personal development as part of professional development. We the adults can begin with our own self-care, mastering the art of attention, and finding a sense of contentment. Some mindfulness in education programs exclusively teach mindfulness to teachers, assuming that once we can work with our own burnout, compassion fatigue, and attention deficit, then our students will naturally benefit from the mindful role models we become (Jennings, 2015; Jennings et al., 2016).

HOW DOES MINDFULNESS WORK?

The field of mindfulness in education is young, but the research is already confirming what thousand of teachers and students are learning firsthand. For teachers mindfulness reduces stress, helps them focus, and makes them more happy (Roeser et al, 2013). Students are more emotionally regulated and attentive, and their learning improves. The classrooms are more peaceful, there are fewer school conflicts, and kids like each other more (Zoogman et al., 2014). These are preliminary results from teaching mindfulness to youth, and research from teaching mindfulness to adults is well established. For adults practicing mindfulness has been shown to positively transform everything from brain architecture to immune function, positive affect, and even gene expression (Tang et al., 2015).

A potent description of mindfulness is from the movie *Kung Fu Panda*, in which the wise old turtle Oogway says, "Yesterday is history, tomorrow is a mystery, but today is a gift. That is why it is called the present." Being mindful is something we have all done a million times, and some people who have never heard of mindfulness are already really good at it. Being mindful means that we are showing up fully for each moment, paying attention with an open heart. We all have mindful moments when we are engaged with our students, and we can really feel the impact we are making. Being mindful is not something we create, it's a natural state of mind we return to when we are settled in our bodies and attuned to the world around us. Often kids are a lot more mindful than we are, absorbed in the wonder of the moment, though they may not be particularly attentive to the specific things we want them to be mindful of.

There is being mindful, and then there are mindfulness exercises. Mindfulness exercises are what we use to strengthen our attention and compassion. We use our breath as a home base of attention that we return to again and again, limiting our distractibility. We call to mind someone who annoys us so that we can work on forgiveness and compassion. The qualities that everyone wants to see their children develop, such as kindness, attention, and emotional balance, can be exercised like muscles. We can isolate a particular quality, such as attention, and use a focusing practice repeatedly so that mindful attention becomes a habitual attitude. The practice of mindfulness helps us build up the percentage of moments in which we are present rather than lost in thought.

We become scientists with our students, studying our own minds. As teachers we can track our stress levels throughout the day, learning when we may need a break or to open our hearts more with certain kids. Students are empowered to examine their behaviors, thought patterns, and relationships. Instead of acting out, they learn to track the subtle emotional triggers in their bodies so that right before they were going to react they are able to pause and take a breath or ask for help.

Doesn't mindfulness sound like a magic pill? The only problem is that it cannot simply be swallowed with a glass of water. The many benefits of mindfulness develop through consistent practice and introspective explorations into our minds, hearts, and bodies. To relax, we need to become aware of our stress and tension. To find peace of mind, we face the chaotic swirl in our brains. To feel happier and content, we may need to feel the anxiousness and sadness in our hearts.

If we simply think of mindfulness as a calming agent for dysregulated and hyperactive students, then we run the risk of using it like a drug or a behavioral modification technique. Mindfulness is not like that "game" where we tell our kids to see who can be quiet the longest. We are not just trying to shut them up so they won't be so difficult to deal with. Mindfulness cannot be the next school curriculum brought in one year and tossed the next. This is not a subject to be forced on students and teachers or to be tested against standards.

Across the world, mindfulness is supporting focus and regulation so that students can ace their math tests and use impulse control. Before we try to push mindfulness on our students, we can join the thousands of teachers who are on their own introspective journeys, becoming leading lights of presence and compassion. Often after taking a mindfulness training, teachers will say that they find an amazing transformation in their classrooms, not from teaching their kids anything but from showing up as a mindful teacher. It's like dropping an ice cube in a cup of hot water and feeling it cool down. Then other teachers and principals get interested. "What are you doing in there? Your class seems so chill." This is the quiet revolution under way. Not a top-down curriculum based educational reform, but an organic, committed group of conscious individuals cultivating our own compassion and presence, slowly and unstoppably rippling into the world.

The Five Realms of Mindful Literacy

Mindfulness is a way of being. It is an open-minded and open-hearted view we can take while chatting with friends, walking to class, or grading papers. Here we explore how to take a mindful view in all of the realms of our lives. We explore how to be mindful of our bodies, minds, hearts, relationships, and with the world all around us. We first gain this wisdom for ourselves and then we will learn to teach youth these five mindful literacies.

PHYSICAL LITERACY

Champion sports teams and Olympic athletes practice mindfulness because they say it helps them relax their stress and slow down their thoughts to enter into a flow state, an experience where they are more present in their bodies and attuned to the world around them. When learning mindfulness, we begin by relaxing and slowing down our busy minds. For our students' minds to be sharp and creative, we need to make sure they are getting their basic physical needs met and feel safe and secure in the classroom. Our first job as teachers is to welcome students into the room and help them feel regulated in the space. Adults begin mindfulness practice the same way. We slow down our usual pace of life and find a state of rest, relaxation, and introspection. Physical literacy lessons help us wake up our senses to gain a feeling of wonder and connection to our bodies and the physical world.

MENTAL LITERACY

Once we are physically regulated and present, we can cultivate our attention. We build our attention muscles by choosing a focus point, such as our breath or the taste of an orange. Then we get to watch the unruliness of our minds, distracted here and there. The practice of mindfulness is to kindly bring attention back again and again to the point of focus. In this way we learn about the mechanics of our minds and master our mental capacity. Young children can learn to watch their thoughts passing like clouds, which is particularly helpful when the thought is one that would get them in trouble if they followed it. As adults, this practice lets us watch our own thoughts with the ability to be not so impulsive and not get caught in the tumble of rumination.

EMOTIONAL LITERACY

Once we have learned the language of sensations and the mechanics of the mind, we can bring them together, learning the language of the heart. We can witness unhealthy thought patterns and learn to uncover the feelings that underlie them. By tracking our stress levels and emotional states, we can build impulse control and emotional regulation. We can also cultivate healthy emotions like empathy, gratitude, and love. We are not suppressing anger or anxiety; rather, we are opening our compassionate awareness to the full spectrum of emotions. An amazing outcome of mindfulness is that when we are fully present with our emotions, happiness, compassion, and gratitude get stronger while feelings such as anger, anxiety, and depression lose their strength. Some of our emotions are very painful, but as we are

present to them, our hearts open wider, and we become more compassionate to ourselves and the world around us.

SOCIAL LITERACY

Having found compassion and regulation, we can become mindfulness
ambassadors, bringing these skills into the world. We can develop empathy
for our friends, family, and eventually even those people who annoy us. We
can use mindfulness to look at our assumptions and start understanding
other perspectives. We can learn to see the world with fresh, empathic,
and understanding eyes. Whether it's in our faculty room, our romantic
relationships, or the social dynamics on the playground, we all have a lot
to learn about empathic communication and social literacy. We are not just
learning to be mindful so that we can find inner peace amidst a warring
world. We are building inner peace to be a model of what is possible and to
work for equality and inclusion for all of our students and community.

GLOBAL LITERACY

We don't need to stop expanding our circle of compassion with our
community. We can gain understanding and care for everyone on the
planet—even the birds, deer, and oceans. By opening our mindful eyes,
we can gain an understanding of the interconnectedness of all things and
the ways our actions affect the world. We can also become mindful enough
to learn how our environments affect our moods and mind states. Often
we don't even realize how the bright fluorescent lights in our classrooms
negatively affect our students and ourselves. With a wider view of how we
impact and are affected by the world, we can take greater responsibility
for our lives. When we open to a global perspective, we expand our
compassion and understanding from our friends and families to all
those billions of beings out there who are striving for safety, health, and
happiness, just like we are.

How to Use This Book

This workbook is aimed at empowering educators to bring mindfulness
and emotional intelligence into their work with youth to positively trans-

form communities and lives. Learning to teach mindfulness in an authentic and effective way has some important steps that we walk through here.

The first section, Beginning with Ourselves, is a mini-mindfulness training. This is an opportunity for adults to cultivate their own self-awareness and inner resources. Before we can be guides for our students, we need to know the terrain ourselves. With personal mindfulness practices, we explore the terrain of our bodies, minds, hearts, society, and ecology. With exercises and recommendations, we have a chance to build a foundational mindfulness practice from which all the rest of our teaching can be built. In this section we learn to use mindfulness when it counts: in the midst of classroom chaos, burnout, and compassion fatigue. We also take time to explore our emotional maturity. Before we teach mindfulness to others, it is indispensable to learn the art of introspection and emotional intelligence so we can be models for our students and not project our own issues onto them.

In the second section, Introducing Mindfulness to Students: Resources and Recommendations, we take the practices we have developed and learn how to embody them with our students. We explore tools for teaching in a mindful way and presenting mindfulness themes to students. We also consider how to structure an environment in which students will feel most relaxed, happy, and able to focus. Then we consider how to apply our mindful presence when teaching students of different age groups, diverse backgrounds, and with trauma and special needs. We can learn how to engage all students and offer mindfulness teachings in a way that students will find fun and engaging.

Our section on Mindfulness Lessons for Students: Classroom Activities, Practices, and Techniques is a full mindfulness-based lesson collection. Before we jump into the curriculum we examine 10 research-based mindfulness objectives. We also look at ways to present mindfulness to students to make it accessible and interesting. We look at the lesson template, which will be used in 25 of the lessons throughout the curriculum. Each lesson contains learning objectives, considerations for teaching to different ages, and other implementation recommendations. The lessons are laid out in a clear progression of five realms of learning literacy. We move from physical literacy to mental literacy, emotional literacy, social literacy, and finally global literacy. It will become clear why it is ordered in this way, since certain practices need to be built on previous capacities. Finally there are five integration lessons that will be helpful in weaving the practices into the school day.

The final section, Integrating Mindfulness: Recommendations, Insights, and Tools, supports us in integrating these teachings into our lives and work. With worksheets and recommendations, we can use this chapter to feel confident bringing this work to our community. There are recommendations for implementation from teachers and mindfulness in education leaders. There are worksheets to create your own mindfulness-based lessons as well as an opportunity to explore presenting mindfulness to our larger communities. In the final section we explore how to integrate mindfulness into our schools fluidly and effectively.

Finding Time for Mindfulness

Often teachers worry that they don't have enough time amidst their lessons to weave in a mindfulness practice in which the kids are just sitting there doing nothing. But once teachers carve out the space—maybe just a few minutes in the beginning of each class—they realize that they get much more done and the students can receive information much better. It's as if we said we didn't want to chew our food before we ate it because it took too much time. We may be able to get the food into our stomachs quicker, but it wouldn't be as healthy or enjoyable. When we take the time to be mindful, we live with greater ease of being, rather than stressfully jumping from one thing to the next.

When scientists scan the brains of people who have been practicing mindfulness intensively for many years, they see a profound integration of brain regions (Vestergaard-Poulsen et al., 2009). Now there is growing research showing that in only eight weeks, beginning mindfulness practitioners had positive transformations in the brain regions correlated with learning, emotion regulation, and self-awareness (Hölzel et al., 2011). Rather than sitting for hours we can begin by taking short pauses often. Mindfulness is not another excuse to beat ourselves up because we aren't exercising enough or eating right. This is not an internal prison sentence.

Eventually we may build to mindfully sitting and breathing for 40 minutes, but at first we can start with digestible and enjoyable lengths of time. Mindfulness can be fun!

I try to find ways to make mindfulness into an engaging game in schools. In one class I came up with a new mindfulness "game" where we were seeing how many sounds we could hear. One third-grade student said abruptly, "That's not a game." We don't want to just call some boring practice a game, we want the students to genuinely find it enthralling. We have to find the way to make mindfulness into a wondrous experience of learning.

Mindfulness needs to be fun and engaging, but we also do need some determination to be able to develop mindful awareness. To cultivate attention and compassion in our fast-paced culture, we need to swim against the stream. There are a million digital distractions, and the news is full of tragedies. Without determined mindfulness practice, it's easy to close down our hearts and lose the rudder of our goals and vision.

We must find the balance in which our practice can be both enjoyable and simultaneously transformative. Maybe we begin by sitting silently every morning for five minutes, holding this as a special time, just for us. If we want we can lie down, sit in the morning sun, or find an ideal cushion to sit on. We make a commitment to ourselves to be still at this time, and slowly we can build moments of mindfulness throughout the day—a moment before lunch to rest and reflect, a moment in the car before we turn the engine on, a moment before we eat, a moment with a loved one. If we don't carve out these times and stick to them, then the old dictum of "nature abhors a vacuum" happens. Those special moments have a way of getting filled with responding to a few messages or rehashing a recent conversation with a colleague. We need to commit to giving ourselves the gift of presence, of spacious moments to return to our breath and our hearts.

We want to weave as many mindful reminders as we can into our days. This means that we regularly pause and recognize the weather patterns in our minds, hearts, and bodies. We can set up reminders, such as every time we get in the shower we remember to feel the water, every time we walk up the stairs of the school we feel the steps, or every time a student enters the room we make eye contact and see them clearly. We want to find mindfulness practices that work for us, ways that we can pause the spinning mind and land in the present moment. Maybe our mindfulness practice is walking by the lake, mindfully staring at lady bugs, or mindfully knitting. The first thing is to find a present-moment endeavor that we enjoy.

Once we find the merit of mindfulness practice in our own direct experience, we can start extending that practice. Throughout this book we explore many mindfulness practices pertaining to the body, mind, heart, relationships, and world. Once we have found a taste for these practices, we can dedicate ourselves to cultivating mindfulness, pushing our own edges to sit longer and look more deeply. In the Beginning with Ourselves section, we have the opportunity to commit to an ongoing mindfulness practice in an accessible and enjoyable way.

Setting Intentions

Our intention is vitally important to set and hold steady when practicing mindfulness and teaching our students. We choose a direction when we set sail and then we hold our compass steady. Even if we are blown off course, which happens regularly, we always remember our destination. Our intention with mindfulness is learning to be ever present and compassionate to what is true in ourselves and supporting our students to cultivate their own presence and compassion. We all want to be more relaxed, focused, and happy in our own lives. We also want our students to gain these indispensable life skills. We can extend our scope of care to hoping that teachers and students around the world can learn to be more mindful, envisioning what it would be like if the next generation of the whole world were raised more mindfully. So let's set our intention as we set sail.

First, how do we hope to be personally transformed by learning the art of mindfulness? Maybe we want to be less reactive, happier, or possibly just able to sleep better. We can write down how we hope that mindfulness will help us in our lives.

Second, what are our hopes and intentions in bringing mindfulness to our students? Maybe we want them to find inner calm, sustain attention, or develop kindness toward ourselves and others. We can write here what effects we hope to see from teaching mindfulness to our students.

Finally, we focus our intention on the larger world. With all the social, environmental, and political turmoil, how do we hope to help the planet by bringing mindfulness to our students? We could say we hope kids finding inner peace could inspire world peace. Let's write down how we hope reading this book and being part of this movement will affect the world.

Beginning with Ourselves

———————

*"People who haven't seen me in years say I exude calm.
Go figure! Mindfulness practice has become routine, like flossing,
but with much more visible benefits. I love the practices,
I love the benefits in how it makes me feel."*
—GREGORY DAVID, ELEMENTARY SCHOOL TEACHER, NEW YORK CITY

———————

WALKING THE MINDFUL TALK

After 15 years in the classroom, Teresa found herself dreading coming to school. She had never had a class with so many dysregulated, stressed-out students. At moments in the day, as she was pulled in every direction by the needs and demands of 25 second-graders, she could feel her heart racing, her emotions swirling, and her mind at the edge of panic. The mindfulness-based stress reduction class she attended taught her to slow down, get some space from her anxious thoughts, and befriend the agitated feelings that were arising in her body. She started feeling as if there was a dysregulated second-grader inside her own heart, and as the panic came, she learned to scoop up that scared inner kid and hold her close.

Amazingly, once she started this practice, not only did she feel a whole lot calmer and more peaceful, but her students seemed to relax with her. The same old chaos would be unraveling after the students returned from PE, and as the Teresa's anxiousness rose, she would stop, drop in, and roll with the feeling. Somehow the students responded by relaxing with her. It was like she had dropped an ice cube into a hot glass of water. Everything chilled out.

As Teresa kept practicing her own mindfulness, not only did it affect her students, the classrooms next door began to take notice. Her colleagues said things like, "Did you give them all happy drugs? Can you teach me how to do that with my kids?" The magic that Teresa learned was that when we take responsibility for our inner transformation, we can have a great effect on the world around us. When we become the peace we want to see in our classroom, the students feel peaceful when they are around us.

I hear Teresa's story over and over again from educators working on their own personal transformation and becoming beacons for others. I also hear another repeating statement from educators. They say, "I keep trying to get my students and colleagues to learn about mindfulness so they will be more calm and happy, but they won't listen." Sometimes it can be isolating for a teacher who has fallen in love with mindfulness and wants to spread the benefits to all the struggling students and staff. However, mindfulness cannot be forced on anyone. Mindfulness is not the next cookie-cutter curriculum fad that we will be forcing on schools. This must be an organic process that begins with our personal development and spreads through genuine interest and openness.

The superintendent may walk into our room and be so blown away that she asks us to teach mindfulness to every educator in the district. Or we may spend our entire teaching career with one classroom that all the kids love coming to as a safe harbor of calm and creative learning although none of the other teachers or administrators take any notice. We can't force it. Taking responsibility for our own lives is incredibly empowering and transformative.

Later in this book we arrive at the curriculum section, in which we will learn the art of teaching mindfulness to youth. Here we begin with personal development before we get into professional development. We can start by realizing that everything we may want to attain with mindfulness is already here. No need to go anywhere or buy something—mindfulness is an inside job. Calmness, happiness, balance, and presence are states of being that we foster within ourselves by simply pausing and tending to our inner worlds. Even without any mindfulness training, we can start now by simply allowing our everyday thoughts, feelings, and sensations to float forward as we take a moment's pause to rest our awareness just enough to witness reality happening in front of us. For a few minutes we can take it all in, noticing the weather patterns of this particular moment. Try it for a few minutes.

In the following lessons we attune to the realms of body, mind, heart, society, and ecology. In any moment of pause and reflection, all five dimensions are happening and affecting us, but without cultivating mindful presence we often miss much of what is happening in our world. We break these five dimensions apart to focus on them separately, and the end goal is to bring them together into an integrated whole.

THE MINDFULNESS LITERACIES

Physical Literacy

Many of us have so many tasks and responsibilities that we rev our brain engines perpetually in fifth gear. When we come to one of those rare pauses in our lives, sitting at a red light or lying in the bath, we forget how to come back to neutral. We end up grinding the gears, our brains spinning even though we finally have found a space of peace to enjoy some precious moments.

By living in third, fourth, or fifth gear, we end up forgetting what neutral even feels like. When we lie down to sleep, our minds are still racing. To come back to neutral, we can begin by finding out what stress gears we are in. To do this, we explore the main stress zones in the body, such as the shoulders, jaws, stomach, and chest. We don't have to try and get rid of the feelings, we just notice how much tightness is there and then bring a sense of kindness and relaxation to them. *Trying* to relax doesn't help—relaxation happens when we stop trying.

PRACTICE: RELAXATION 101

Lying down in a comfortable position, we take a moment to close our eyes and get a general sense of what is happening in our bodies, as if we're checking the inner weather patterns. Notice if there is agitation, calmness, happiness, sadness, pain; whatever is noticed, we can be aware of without needing to change anything.

Now we sweep our awareness through our bodies, noticing any tension on the in breath and relaxing on the out breath. Starting with our heads and our faces, we can notice if there is any tension in the muscles. If we notice tension, we can tighten the muscles a little more while breathing in and then letting go of the tension with a big sigh on the exhale.

Then we check our neck and shoulder muscles. See if there is any tension in this area on the in-breath, noticing tension, tightening a little more, and then releasing and melting the muscles into the ground on the out breath.

Try these same mindful inhales and relaxed exhales throughout the body, spending a minute or so in each zone. Move to the arms and hands, then the heart, belly, down through the back, hips, bottom, and all the way down the legs and feet. Moving through our bodies, we identify any tension and accentuate the tension on the inhales, relaxing and releasing with long exhales.

Once we have moved from our heads to our feet, we can continue for a few minutes, breathing into our whole bodies like big balloons, noticing any tension on the inhales and releasing any stress down into the ground on the exhales.

BRINGING IT ALL BACK HOME

When we are ready to get up, we can commit to staying aware of the tension and relaxation in our bodies. As we turn on our cell phones or hop in the car, we can see how our bodies respond. Do the shoulders and chest tighten up? We can remember that our breath is with us wherever we go and as we learn to track our stress levels we can regulate with our relaxing body breaths.

Mental Literacy

While I was leading a mindfulness training for teachers on the Pacific cliffs of California, an elementary school principal asked me a prescient question. "Just feeling my breath is really boring, why shouldn't I imagine myself down by the ocean watching the dolphins and whales splashing in the waves?" I also loved watching the whales and dolphins playing all week, so I appreciated the question. I replied, "It sounds like you are really loving being down by the ocean." She looked at me like I had caught her with her hand in the cookie jar. "Actually it's been really frustrating. Everybody is spotting the whales but I'm so caught up worrying about my family back home I keep missing them!"

When we are easily distracted, we have trouble staying present, even to the most precious things in our lives, such as our families, a beautiful sunset, or a delicious meal. Our capacity to focus is like a muscle we can exercise. A great place to exercise focus muscles is with our breath as a central hub, sitting quietly with as few external distractions as possible. As we build our focus, we learn to love the seemingly boring experience of breath coursing in and out of our bodies. As we build this capacity we become more present for the whales and dolphins splashing, for the smiles of our children, and for all the seemingly mundane mysteries of our lives. This principal wrote me after the training saying, "Once I learned how to appreciate the stillness of sitting and feeling my breath then I was able to let go of all the thoughts and really enjoy walking by the ocean. Then when I got home I found I was able to really be present with my family."

PRACTICE: BUILDING ATTENTION MUSCLES

Finding an upright and settled sitting posture, we can set an attitude for our practice of focus and relaxation. We can begin with a few long breaths, where our spines stretch tall with each inhale and then our muscles and bones relax down into the earth on each exhale. Now we can let our breath become natural, and we can focus on the physical experience of the four points of the breath.

1. Bring awareness to the feeling of the whole inhale.
2. Note what it feels like when the lungs are full right before the exhale.
3. Bring awareness to the physical experience of the whole exhale.
4. Note what it feels like when the breath is empty before the inhale.

Our breath organically moves through these four points, and we can develop a focused awareness on the sensations and experience of each breath. Eventually as our attention builds, we notice the intricacies of the breath movement. We can let go of focusing on the specific points of breath and stay finely attuned to each breath like watching waves crash and recede over and over.

Our focus may wander at moments. Don't worry about it. All minds meander. Our job is to begin gaining a greater understanding of the mechanics and movement of our minds. When the attention gets distracted from the points of breath, we can simply experience where we have wandered. We may go into thought, strong sensations, or emotions, and then we gently return the attention back to the breath. By diligently bringing the awareness back again and again to the breath, we are building our attention while gaining insight into the mechanics of our minds.

BRINGING IT ALL BACK HOME

At the end of our mindfulness practice, the practice does not really end. As we move through our day, we have new opportunities every moment to watch the way our awareness gets distracted from the task at hand and how we learn to bring it gently back. We can remember to have fun engaging ever more closely with our students, the food we eat, and every breath we breathe.

Emotional Literacy

With kindergarten students, I begin heartfulness practice by saying, "Let's all give ourselves a big hug." No problem for five-year-olds. They wrap their arms around themselves and say all types of sweet things like, "May it be my birthday every day!" What's a little harder for young ones is when I ask them to look at their classmates and send compassionate messages to each other. The younger we are, the more self-love we seem to have, but it can take a while to cultivate kindness toward others.

Adults seem to need to work backward from the kindergarteners. Educators particularly have genuine care and compassion toward kids. That's probably a big part of why we stepped into this profession in the first place. What can be much harder is offering ourselves the same kindness and care. It may not come as easily for us to wrap our arms around ourselves and wish for sweet things.

When we send out so much compassion and nurturing to others but forget our own self-care, we get burned out. We develop compassion fatigue and can end up feeling exhausted and even resentful. "Why am I always taking care of everyone and no one's taking care of me?" So here we open the gates of compassion toward our kids, as we already know how to do, and then turn this kind stare back in toward ourselves. We can learn how to build our own reservoirs of care so that we are overflowing with kindness for others without exhausting our inner resources.

PRACTICE: SELF-COMPASSIONATE

Notice how the breath naturally rises and falls in the chest. We don't need to breathe a particular way—simply notice the breath expanding and contracting in the lungs, however it organically moves. We can keep the attention on the heart area, feeling the sensations and emotions in the chest with each inhale and bringing a sense of relaxation and softening to the heart on each exhale.

Now we can picture a child we care about. When we imagine them, it's really easy for us to smile and feel a genuine sense of care. Picture them doing whatever they love to do and see what the heart feels like as the child is so happy. We can notice what it feels like in our hearts when we genuinely care for another.

Now we can turn this compassionate gaze in on ourselves. On every inhale we can notice however our hearts are feeling. Maybe our hearts feel happy, maybe sad; whatever we notice we can simply breathe in with awareness. As we exhale, we can shine the same compassionate stare toward our hearts. If the heart is happy, we really let it taste the sweetness of happiness. If our hearts are sad, we can feel compassion for our own pain. With every inhale we notice what is happening in our hearts and with every exhale we offer ourselves kindness and compassion.

BRINGING IT ALL BACK HOME

As we navigate through the rest of our day, we can continue to stay close to our hearts. When something delightful happens, we rejoice in the sweetness of the feelings that arise. When something happens that is frustrating, we tend to our hearts as if we were caring for a crying child. Without trying to hold on too tightly to the sweet feelings and without trying to push away the uncomfortable ones, we practice keeping our hearts open through the inevitable waves of our day.

Social Literacy

We begin our mindfulness practice by looking inside, relaxing, offering self-care, and getting to know the nature of our own minds. From this grounded and empathic space, we learn to become ambassadors of mindfulness for our students, colleagues, and family members. We do this by taking the presence we have cultivated and attuning to what is happening with the people all around us.

One of the most profound gifts of mindfulness is that it can help us witness our thought patterns and realize which of them may be unconscious assumptions or biases. Often we go through our lives with judgments toward others that have been handed down from our families and societies. It takes some real witness capacity to step back and inquire into our minds around what is true and what is a toxic leftover which would be healthy to release.

When we can see through our assumptions, we see people as they actually are. We see the ways people struggle as well as how they shine. This understanding is the key to compassion. When we learn to see others as they truly are, we give them the gift of being seen. Isn't that what we all truly want—to be seen and accepted exactly as we are?

PRACTICE: OPENING TO EMPATHY

We can begin by letting our bodies relax and returning to the four-part breath. With each breath we cultivate some stillness and focus. Now bring to mind a recent experience with a student that was frustrating. We can picture it in our minds like a video replaying the incident. As we picture this incident, we can notice which thoughts are correlated with it. See if there are any judgments passing through the mind.

As we keep picturing this student, we bring our awareness to our emotions and sensations. Is the jaw tight? Is the heart heavy? Observe how picturing this scene affects our bodies. Take a few breaths, noticing where any tension or discomfort is on the inhale and relaxing and releasing on the exhale. Try this a few times until there is a sense of stillness.

Now picture the student again, but this time hold our hearts open to them. As we picture the student we can say to ourselves:

Just like me, this student has so much going on inside.

Just like me, this student wants to be happy.

Just like me, this student struggles.

Just like me, this student wants to find a sense of balance.

We can say all types of empathic phrases, realizing how the student has so much going on inside just like we do. We stay interested to see what it feels like in our hearts to be empathic even when we are frustrated.

BRINGING IT ALL BACK HOME

Whenever we experience frustration toward our students, colleagues, or family members, we can practice this exercise. We notice the ways people trigger us and take a moment to look inside. We witness our thoughts, feel our feelings, and see if we can work our empathy muscles. When we practice in this way, we learn to respond with greater composure, nonjudgment, and kindness.

Global Literacy

Let's take a moment to expand our mindful view and consider where we are. Whether we are living in a sprawling metropolis or on a rural farm, we are in a completely dependent relationship with our environment. The food we eat, the air we breathe, the birds we hear, the seasons we live through all have a profound effect on how we live and who we are.

In the same way we looked deeply into our breath and emotions, we can look into our world. We can begin by asking ourselves questions such as

What direction am I facing right now?

Where does my water come from?

Where does the electricity I'm using come from, and what was it made from?

Where does my garbage go?

Who lived on this land 500 years ago?

What is the cultural demographic where I live and how did each culture come here?

Why would we want to know this? First, we get to truly appreciate the elements that keep us alive every day. We develop gratitude for the trees that we rely on for oxygen and the rains that bring water for our bodies and life to the soil. Asking these questions helps us be more aware of the natural and social Earth we live on. By becoming more mindful of our world, we develop reverence for natural systems and compassion for the interconnected web we are part of. We can even learn to bring health and balance to our surroundings, which will bring health and balance back to our own bodies and communities.

PRACTICE: OPEN AWARENESS

Find a relaxed sitting position and bring attention to the breath. We can imagine ourselves as mindful meteorologists feeling the swirling breath like wind entering in through the nose, filling the chest and belly, before releasing and flowing back out through the nostrils. Feel the inner weather pattern as it moves with every in breath and out breath.

After a couple minutes of feeling the inner weather patterns, we turn our attention to the outside world by listening to the patterns of sound. We don't have to do anything to hear the myriad sounds arriving in our ears. We can sit back and listen to the sounds appearing and subsiding. We also notice the field of silence from which the sounds arise and pass away again and again.

After a couple minutes we can shuttle our awareness inside once again to be aware of the breath rising and falling, feeling our inner world. After a minute we shift again to the outer world, listening to the sounds that we are immersed in like fish in the sea. Then we bring awareness to the inner world and the outer world simultaneously, aware of the breath, emotions, sensations, sounds, smells and opening the awareness to everything all at once. Let awareness flow easily from one phenomenon to the next, opening a wide view in which all senses can be seen.

BRINGING IT ALL BACK HOME

We can practice this open awareness in everyday life, when we listen to the wind, the birds, the cars, the chattering children, the symphony of the particular place we inhabit. We are not practicing mindfulness so that we will be unaffected by the chaos of the outside world, we are practicing so that we can feel the full effect with an open heart and an open mind, responding with intelligence and care. The more interested we get in our natural environment, the more we will learn and the more care we will take.

INNER ASSESSMENT WORKSHEET

The research on the benefits of mindfulness shows how it supports stress reduction, happiness, emotional regulation, kindness, and attention. But don't just listen to the experts. We can study the effects of mindfulness on our own lives, tracking how well the practices are working on our minds, hearts, bodies, and relationships.

The benefits will only come if we take the time to practice. At the end of every day, you can use this worksheet and write down what mindfulness practices you did, when you did them, and for how long. Then fill in the questions noting state of mind and mood. With this, you can begin to recognize how these practices affect you. You can dedicate yourself to practicing every day and use this worksheet as inner laboratory research. You will see the benefits of mindfulness firsthand and then be empowered to commit to your own practice.

INNER ASSESSMENT

What practices did you do today, when did you do them, and for how long?

_____

_____

_____

Stress Reduction: What was your stress level today?

STRESS MESS				NEUTRAL				CHILLING	
1	2	3	4	5	6	7	8	9	10

Focused Attention: How well were you able to focus today?

SPACED OUT				NEUTRAL				LASER	
1	2	3	4	5	6	7	8	9	10

Empathy: How nice do you think you were to people today?

MEAN				NEUTRAL				KIND	
1	2	3	4	5	6	7	8	9	10

Resilience: How balanced were you today amidst adversity?

STRUGGLING				NEUTRAL				GRACEFUL	
1	2	3	4	5	6	7	8	9	10

Self-Compassion: How kind were you to yourself today?

HARSH				NEUTRAL				LOVING	
1	2	3	4	5	6	7	8	9	10

Contentment: How balanced was your mood today?

CHAOTIC				NEUTRAL					HAPPY
1	2	3	4	5	6	7	8	9	10

Open-Mindedness: How aware were you today of the world around you?

MINDLESS				NEUTRAL					ATTUNED
1	2	3	4	5	6	7	8	9	10

Emotional Self-Regulation: How was your impulse control today?

RECKLESS				NEUTRAL					VIGILANT
1	2	3	4	5	6	7	8	9	10

Metacognition: How busy was your mind today?

FRENZIED				NEUTRAL					TRANQUIL
1	2	3	4	5	6	7	8	9	10

Executive Functioning: How much drama did you get caught up in today?

CALAMITY				NEUTRAL					PEACEFUL
1	2	3	4	5	6	7	8	9	10

Cognitive Flexibility: How easy were transitions for you today?

DISCOMBOBULATING			NEUTRAL					SMOOTH	
1	2	3	4	5	6	7	8	9	10

SETTING UP A SUCCESSFUL MINDFULNESS PRACTICE

For many of us, if we sit down and try to silently watch our breath for 45 minutes, much of the time will be a practice in frustration. The frenzy of mental chatter alone may leave us feeling incompetent and rather turned off by this whole mindfulness endeavor. In this way, our brains may link up mindfulness with annoyance and self-criticism.

Instead of setting up an experience of frustration, let's set ourselves up for success. We can approach mindfulness practice within a personally accessible range that feels enjoyable, clarifying, and empowering.

We can think of mindfulness practice as a plant that needs a particular amount of sun, water, and soil. The elements that feed the growth and blossoming of our mindful awareness are as simple as the posture in which we sit, the intentions we create, the support we call in, and the way we schedule our sittings.

There are four main postures in mindfulness practice: sitting, walking, standing, and lying down. The intention is to be mindfully aware of every posture, including washing the dishes posture, writing on the blackboard posture, and even arguing with our spouse posture. The following recommendations are specifically for mindful sitting posture. It's helpful at first to have as little distraction as possible so we can really focus. Therefore, a quiet, still, sitting practice can be a good place to start. We can build attention with minimal stimuli before we eventually maintain our dialed attention in the midst of an all-school assembly.

Making Space

Our houses have designated places where we feed ourselves, clean our bodies, and rest. Similarly we can create an intentional space to foster our mindful awareness. Of course the goal of mindfulness is to bring an open-hearted presence to every space we occupy, and to build this capacity we create a mindful sitting spot that we return to again and again as a safe harbor. If we have enough space, we can create a mindfulness room in our house, or we can simply set up a spot in the corner of the bedroom. We can put flowers and pictures of inspiring teachers or artwork. When we have set up our spot with beauty and significance, we are giving ourselves a gift every time we sit down.

We can also create a sit spot out in nature. If there is a nice bench in a park near our home or a quiet spot in the forest, we can return there to be still and listen to the ecosystem. We can come regularly enough to watch the seasons changing and the migratory birds coming and going. Maybe we will learn something about nature and the nature of our own minds.

We can also create a safe harbor in our classrooms. Often teachers feel overwhelmed by the idea of setting aside 20 or even 5 minutes to practice mindfulness, but if we set up a mindfulness spot in the room, we can simply come back to it for 30 seconds several times a day. The spot is a reminder. We can put a poem we love, a plant, something that will remind us to slow down, take a breath, and return to our hearts. If we have time at lunch or during a break, we could find 10 or 20 minutes to practice breathing or compassion in our spot.

Setting the Time

How long and how often should we sit? What is most important at first is setting up a practice that feels within our capability. If you are new to mindfulness and have some external ideal that you are supposed to sit for 40 minutes twice a day, there is a good chance you will not be able to meet that goal. Then you will be battling against yourself. Try to check in and see what would be realistic. If 10 minutes every morning feels manageable, then go for that. We can always increase the time if you are feeling inspired and want to go deeper into the practice.

We can adjust the duration of our practice and the time of day as we go. Remember to think of mindfulness practice like a houseplant that needs a particular amount of sun and water. Try sitting in the morning for 15 minutes and see how the system responds. Was that too much time? Try sitting at night. Was there too much tiredness then? Maybe we have kids, maybe we're a morning person, maybe we have to wake up at 5:00 a.m. to commute—we can find a time or times in our particular day to commit to a doable duration of practice.

If we decide to commit to a practice, we should set ourselves up to succeed. Mindfulness is not a punishment; it's a gift. We can plan our mindfulness times right into a calendar so we can be reminded. We can set timers throughout the day that can be short moments of mindfulness. When the chime rings, we can take a few mindful breaths. Once we begin to schedule these mindful moments in our day, we begin to remember to take unplanned moments of pause. As we're walking down the street or while we're in the shower, we can pause and enjoy the moment.

Finding Your Posture

The following is a foundation for a mindful sitting practice. When we set up the posture, we create a foundation on which our awareness grows. Think of a three-legged stool and its sturdy design. Make sure to have three points of contact with the Earth. Sometimes early practitioners sit cross-legged with their knees up. This is sure to lead to back pain. If we can sit with our bottoms on a cushion and our knees on the ground this is great, but since most of us are habituated to sitting in chairs, our bodies will struggle to do this. We can always sit in a chair or on a sitting bench with our legs tucked under. Whatever posture we take, make sure that either the knees or feet are planted on the ground and the bottom is firmly placed. If the body has special needs or a lot of pain, lie down or stand. We need to find a posture that is within our range while remaining aware of our contact with the Earth.

In a seated posture, it's helpful to have the pelvis slightly tilted forward so the spine doesn't collapse back. The chest naturally opens and we can bring awareness to the spine lifting up through the top of the head.

If sitting in a chair, make sure to sit a little forward and not lean back against the chair. If the body starts collapsing or leaning back, there is a good chance the mind will lose its alertness and things will become foggy.

The hands can rest on the lap or knees. No need to hold them a particular way, but it is better not to let them just flop to the sides. Bring a sense of conscious awareness to however they are placed.

While practicing, we may want to let our eyes be half open or just little slits. This reminds us to hold our awareness half inside and half outside. We are relaxing and simultaneously fully aware. If it is too distracting to have the eyes slightly open, it's fine to let them be closed.

Every time you begin a practice, remember to set up the posture in this way. Bring conscious awareness to the whole body. Take a few breaths, and on each inhale feel tall and focused like a redwood tree. On the exhale relax and let go down into the Earth. This way we can set ourselves up with a solid somatic foundation for practice.

Setting an Intention

After setting up a posture, it is crucial to bring into mind and heart what the purpose of our practice is. Why are we doing this? This is a good question to ask every day and in every practice. Why do we want to focus our minds, relax our bodies, and open our hearts?

We can get in touch with the profound importance of this practice. We are working hard to be more present for our own lives and for the benefit of our students and the world. There is so much chaos in our minds, our relationships, and our society, and we can remember the intention of this practice as an antidote.

Bringing in Support

We notice once we begin to practice how supportive a community and a teacher can be for our further development. If we have a mindfulness center in our area, it is invaluable to gather with this group. We may also set up a group of teachers that sits once a week or gather for 10 minutes before class every morning to set a mindful course for the day. When we practice with community, it can feel like we are in a flock of geese gaining air current support from the group effort. If we do not have an accessible mindfulness community, there are great teachers and teachings online and plenty of recorded and written mindfulness practices.

Whether or not we have a community, we can begin our practice with a moment of connecting inwardly with our teachers and the mindfulness community at large. After setting intentions, we can bring in our beloved community, elders, teachers, and role models. We picture these figures circling us and looking at us with benevolent eyes. We can picture our wise grandparents, inspirational figures, and possibly our dearest friends. We can bring in all the people whom we feel supported by and whom we look to as wise teachers. Setting ourselves up with these benevolent supporters creates a net of support for our practice.

Establishing Focus

Once we have set our posture, made our intention, and drawn in our circle of support, we can develop attention. There are many points of attention we can use at the beginning of practice, such as the breath, the sensations in the body, sounds, or focusing with the eyes on an object. At first we probably end up noticing the distracted nature of our mind and our perpetual need to herd the awareness back to the stable of our attention. In the mess of our daily distracted minds, we begin mindfulness practice by stabilizing awareness using a focus point, often the breath, to kindly bring the mind into alignment.

It may be that as we begin our minds will stay on the object of attention 25 percent of the time and 75 percent lost in thought. Attention will build with dedicated persistence until the presence to distraction ratio is more like 50:50, and eventually we aim to stay focused on the object of attention at least 75 percent of the time.

Once the muscles of attention are built, we can evolve our practice from focusing on one object to opening and entering the flow of awareness. We could try this right now by staring at an object in our visual field for a minute. Then we can open our field of vision so that we are aware of everything simultaneously—kind of like spacing out, but doing it consciously. We notice that the original object is still there, but now it is part of a larger landscape. Preliminarily we build our attention on one object of attention and then we learn the art of opening to the larger field of awareness that contains breath, sound, emotion, and thought; our focus expands to embrace everything all at once.

Framing Practice

As the session comes to a close, remember that mindfulness does not need to end. We can open our eyes mindfully, check our phone mindfully, do whatever we do mindfully. We can gain a continuity of practice flowing from our sitting posture directly into every nook and cranny of our life.

Remember at the end of each practice to appreciate whatever arose in the time we were sitting. A successful practice isn't measured by how peaceful we were or by how few thoughts we had. If there is a measure to the progression of our practice, it is how accepting and empathic we can be to whatever it is that arises within our field of awareness. So at the end of sitting, we can thank every visitor that entered our awareness, whether those visitors were anger, anxiousness, peacefulness, or joy. We can appreciate the capacity for staying present and opening to what is. Then we can make a commitment to live the rest of the day carrying this interested, empathic presence into whatever we do.

SETTING UP A MINDFULNESS PRACTICE WORKSHEET

In this workbook we actually need to put in some work. To build our attention muscles and cultivate compassion, we have to commit to nurturing the soil that can grow these seeds. To do this, we embark on a five-week mindfulness exploration. Don't worry, this isn't some huge commitment that will leave you resenting the fact you ever picked up this book. We are creating a formula for ourselves that will be enjoyable and accessible. We track how the practices are affecting us; most people find that the practices actually help them feel like they have more time in their lives and that they are less stressed when they make the time for mindfulness.

You have read through the *Mindfulness Lessons for Teachers* and *How to Set up a Personal Practice* sections. Now we can commit to a five-week program, practicing each lesson at least once a day for an entire week. We may practice for 10 minutes each day or build up to forty minutes twice a day if we have time and capacity.

Week One: Physical Literacy: Deep Relaxation

Week Two: Mental Literacy: Focusing Muscles

Week Three: Emotional Literacy: Compassionate Heart

Week Four: Social Literacy: Communication Skills

Week Five: Global Literacy: Natural Awareness

SETTING UP A MINDFULNESS PRACTICE

What is the minimum time you are committing to sitting each day and which times of day will you practice?

_____
_____
_____
_____
_____
_____

Where will your mindful sitting spots be, and how will you set them up?

_____
_____
_____
_____
_____

What sitting posture will work best for you and what cushion or chair will you use?

_____
_____
_____
_____
_____

What is your intention and hope for committing to this practice?

_____

_____

_____

_____

_____

_____

What are some obstacles that may get in the way of your meeting your goal, such as getting bored or people interrupting you?

_____

_____

_____

_____

_____

What do you need to navigate through these obstacles?

_____

_____

_____

_____

_____

Who are some allies for you in your practice? (These may be friends to sit with in person and others may be mentors to picture mentally.)

_____

_____

_____

_____

_____

_____

MINDFULNESS RECOMMENDATIONS FROM TEACHERS

Mindful Education and Social Emotional Learning Group, with Linda Lantieri and Daniel Rechtschaffen

Participant Comments

One thing that you do regularly to cultivate your own inner life

> Go on walks, specifically walks without a clear destination or agenda in mind.
> My main mindfulness practice at the moment is gardening and trimming roses.
> Time spent with my dog, walking in nature.
> Mindfully setting up my classroom. Mindfully sit a few minutes before the kids arrive.
> I like to practice mindfulness on the subway.
> I have a gratitude practice with a friend and every day we check in to see what we're grateful for.
> Savoring the moments throughout the day that are heartfelt—for example, when putting my five-year-old to bed every night. That moment is sweet and special and I think back to it when my mind gets busy.
> Preparing simple, delicious foods for dinner.
> During my commute, I use that time to be mindful and notice the surroundings around me and listen to soft music and pay attention to the environment around me, instead of listening to the radio.

> Noticing those moments of presence when I'm interacting with someone. Savoring the connection, even when responding to emails.

> Arrive early to work, get a cup of tea, and read a quote from one of my inspirational quote books. This inspires me to start the day in a positive way.

> After the Super Bowl I packed up my TV and put it in the closet, and now I find myself noticing—well what am I going to do? I pet the cat more. I started playing the banjo more every night. And I'm appreciating the slowness.

> I live on a farm. Being around my animals brings me to the present moment.

> When I step into a building, I notice where I am and I pay attention. Noticing that I've transitioned from outside to inside. I do that every morning when I get to school. The same thing at the end of my workday. I step out and notice the different parts of nature. In every transition I take a moment to be where I am.

> Delight in noticing how my body feels when I first wake up in the morning, noticing the vibrations, slowly stretching and taking a few moments to be back in my body.

> When I arrive home in the driveway, before I go inside I sit in the car for a few minutes, take a few deep breaths, and think about my day . . . and it grounds me before ending my day.

THE ART OF INTROSPECTION

The following is an invitation to learn the art of introspection so that we can become examples for our students of emotional maturity. When teaching emotional intelligence lessons, I often ask kids, "Have you ever done something and then later wished you hadn't done it?" Every child raises their hand, as all of us would as well. We are all driven by forces that are sometimes out of our control. Whether we get angry and say something we wish we hadn't or succumb to an addictive pattern we can't resist, we all fall off the horse sometimes.

The only way to develop emotional maturity is to open up the door to our emotions and gain a respectful relationship with the great forces within. Anxiety, shame, jealousy—these emotions can be overwhelming and distort the way we see the world. What seems counterintuitive to some is that trying to control or push away the emotions only makes them more unruly. As the saying goes, "You have to feel it to heal it." By opening to and honoring our emotions, we eventually ride the waves of joy and sorrow.

Introspection

Every day, we live inside our own bodies and minds. Though that's not a revelation, one might think that since we spend so much time in here we would really want to get to know the inner operating manual. In fact, what could be more important? Being introspective means looking inside at our emotions, thoughts, personality structures, and everything else we experience. We are opening the hood and tinkering around with the engine, learning how we work, and hopefully optimizing the inner mechanics.

Mindfulness is a direct way of becoming introspective. We use mindfulness to look into a mirror at our own minds. We slow down the usual frenzy of thoughts and observe the dynamics at work within. Mindfulness is an inquiry practice. We are inquiring into the nature of our minds. The underlying question is, "Who am I?" Are we our thoughts? Are we our bodies? Are we our emotions? There isn't an exact answer to any of these questions. What happens when we look inside and inquire is that we cultivate a deepening relationship, a friendliness, with ourselves.

Parts of Self

As we look inside, we will have our own discoveries of personality styles and psychological strategies. We also have some universal human experiences we are bound to find. There are particular emotions we all seem to share, like anger, joy, fear, and sadness. It's as if we are driving down the road and we have all these parts of ourselves in the van fighting over the steering wheel. We have scared little kid parts, perfectionist parts, peacemaker parts, and excited cheerleader parts. The problem is that sometimes the scared child part of us gets behind the wheel, instead of being safely secured in a car seat.

The aim of introspection is to learn how to organize our inner world in a healthy way. Each part is there for a reason and cannot be expelled. Anger is a need to be valued and respected. Sadness is a need to feel authentic loss and grief. Fear is our protector, keeping us safe. What we can learn to do with mindfulness is not get so enmeshed in shame or anxious feelings and witness the parts with presence and care. The intention is not to get rid of emotions but to experience them fully without getting lost in them. When we can do this, we learn so much from our emotions.

Vulnerability

By its very nature, introspection is a vulnerable operation. When we look inside, we see aspects of ourselves that are painful. We all have psychologically protective patterns, strategies, and defenses to feel safe and secure in a world that is sometimes tragic. As we slow down and look inside, we are forced to feel some of the stress and emotion that we have been postponing or defending against. It's vulnerable to see the imperfect, work-in-progress parts of ourselves. But that's who we are—beautiful and broken works in progress. The more we accept ourselves as we are and allow ourselves to be vulnerable, the more real we are and the less we have to hide.

Often our vulnerabilities can become problematic if we keep them suppressed for too long. Some people grew up in families where it wasn't acceptable to express sadness. Parents may have said, "Be a big girl and don't cry." Growing up in an environment like this could easily lead to suppressing sadness. In this example sadness would be stuffed into the shadow. We may always put on a happy face, but deep inside there is authentic sadness lingering that could easily turn into depression or cause other problems down the road. Authentic emotions cannot be fully extinguished and have a disturbing effect if they are not given air. Sadness is just one example; some of us push anger into the shadow or maybe even happiness if our family told us to be serious and not too silly.

Projection

To understand projection, think of certain days when we feel really great. Everyone seems to be smiling and the whole world has a special glow. Other times, when we feel dragged down by the weight of the world, everyone looks menacing, and the whole world is gloomy and annoying. Of course it is not that the world has changed, but that we project our inner state onto it.

Awareness of projections becomes incredibly important in our work with students. We may have had an argument with our spouse in the morning and feel really irritated. When we start class, we find ourselves easily annoyed and agitated by the students. If we are able to remember to be introspective, we can realize that our own emotions may be overlaid onto the students. Another example could be that we are uncomfortable expressing sadness. When a child comes into class and starts crying, it would make us anxious and our instinct would be to make them stop crying. We project our shadows onto those around us, unconsciously putting our own fears and frustrations onto them. With mindfulness we can discern when we are projecting and catch ourselves in the act.

Becoming Conscious

It's important to realize that we all have our vulnerabilities, our shadow material, and that we project it on those around us. It's just how we work. The way not to project our vulnerabilities out onto others is to become conscious of what's happening inside and tending to what is unresolved within. As we tend to our sadness and anxiety, we build our capacity to be present to that which is vulnerable. With introspection we realize what is going on inside, and though it may be vulnerable we open our hearts to all of ourselves.

When we can be present with our vulnerabilities, we can be more present to the vulnerabilities in others as well. When we can accept our own sadness, then when students are sad we can be more empathic and understanding. When a class is really anxious about a big test, we usually feel the anxiety as well. If we feel the anxiety in our own bodies, breathing in with care and relaxing, then we will be the life raft for the students to hold onto. They will see that we can feel anxiety, anger, sadness, or whatever intense emotion is happening and not get spun by the experience. We model for them that we have a mature relationship with our own emotions. When we turn our ship of awareness into the storm of our emotions, we navigate the seas of life and then become an example of courageous authenticity for the students to follow.

Modeling

We begin teaching mindfulness by being mindful. We keep an empathic eye open to our students even when they are driving us crazy. We learn to focus on our students and the task at hand even when there are many distractions. We feel our insecurities and discombobulated emotions and develop self-care, being kind to ourselves and modeling how to be strong and authentic. Rather than just telling students to pay attention, be empathic, and self-regulated, we teach them by embodying the practices.

Kids do as we do more than as we say. Rather than telling them how we want them to be, embodying those same characteristics without even talking about it can have a much greater effect. Researchers trying to understand how to support healthy eating habits for kids created three groups of nine-year-old students to try different strategies to see what would actually change habitual eating patterns. The first was a control group with no intervention. The second had regular lectures on how the children should eat more fresh fruit in their diet. In the third group the teachers didn't say a word about diet but always had fresh fruit around the room and would model healthy diet by eating apples regularly.

The study showed that the class receiving lectures and the one where the teachers modeled healthy eating both ended up developing a healthier diet than did the control group. After six months, the class that had received lectures went back to their usual ways, but the class that had received modeling had maintained a new healthy eating lifestyle (Perikkou et al., 2013).

The impact of modeling is immense. If we tell our students to pay attention but then distractedly check our phones throughout the day, the students will take in a lesson of distraction. If we yell at our students to be relaxed, they will learn aggression rather than regulation. We are the teachers, but we are also the lessons.

BECOMING OUR OWN TEACHERS WORKSHEET

We all have our own repeating words of wisdom for our students. If we listened to our wise refrains, we may sound a lot like motivational speakers. I hear elementary school teachers repeating, "Be kind to yourself and others." Middle school teachers say, "Don't compare yourself to others. You are perfect just the way you are." High school teachers say, "You are in control of your own life."

BECOMING OUR OWN TEACHERS

If we turn these affirmations inward and say them to ourselves, we realize we may need to hear these statements just as much as the students. Let's try this now. We can write in the spaces below some of the common words of wisdom we find ourselves repeating to our students.

_____

_____

_____

_____

_____

_____

Read the list slowly, stopping after each statement, closing your eyes, and feeling how deeply you can trust the words that have been spoken. If the statement is "Be kind to yourself," how kind do you actually feel toward yourself? Take a few breaths with each statement and see if you can really let it sink in and trust the truth of what is being said.

_____

_____

_____

_____

_____

_____

Introducing Mindfulness

Resources and Recommendations

"We all desperately need ways to pause and calm ourselves down, especially those of us who teach in and live in trauma-ridden communities. Mindfulness gives me a way (when I can remember) to take a pause before, or as, I am about to lose it. Practicing mindfulness in front of my students—even if it is just me practicing it—models for them that adults sometimes need to pause, and are willing to admit it, willing to be vulnerable with them. Inviting them to practice with me gives them a taste of that moment of peace, of letting down their guard and resting. Once they feel it, they can ask for it when they need it, and remind me to take it when they sense that I need it. It's a way for us to be real together, and to be on equal footing, in a way that is somewhat rare in public education."

—DIANE R. BLOCH, MIDDLE SCHOOL TEACHER, CALIFORNIA

Up to now we have been exploring mindfulness as an inner art form and a way to be in relationship with the world. In this part we explore how to make these inner arts accessible to our students. All subjects are important, and in teaching mindfulness we are particularly inviting students into a path of self-discovery. How we set up these mindfulness lessons, how we engage the students, and how we introduce the topics are art forms unto themselves.

We don't want to approach mindfulness lessons with a structure that uses testing, grading, and memorization. This may be very different than the way we run other subjects. We need to demarcate mindfulness as a special time and space in which students are not learning some preset concept but are actually taking their own initiative to learn for themselves. In mindfulness we are more like learning companions than teachers. We set up a learning laboratory in which we support students to study their own minds, hearts, and relationships.

What we explore in this part is how to create conditions in which students will feel engaged and excited by mindfulness. We need to be wary not to teach mindfulness in a way that is going to seem boring or controlling. If we tell kids to close their eyes for 10 minutes and watch their breath, without any other explanation, they will equate mindfulness with this profoundly frustrating task. Their brains will link up the experience of sitting for 10 minutes, completely annoyed with mindfulness.

We explore how to engage all students in the practices of mindfulness. On some level the foundational practices of mindfulness are the same for everyone. Breathing, regulating anger, mindfully eating a raisin—pretty much everyone will resonate with these practices, and all we need to do is find language, stories, and teaching strategies that work for the specific group. The following are recommendations for how to skillfully bring our inner mindfulness practices into the classrooms.

MINDFUL TEACHING TOOLS

Here we explore some important themes in how to teach mindfully. Once we have cultivated our own mindfulness practice, how do we embody these teaching in the classroom? If we look mindfully at the ways we teach, are there any shifts we want to make? The following suggestions are principles that we can use in embodying a mindful teaching style. As we develop our own mindfulness practice and experiment with teaching mindfulness to students, we will find our own way and build our skills. Here are some basic tools for the journey.

Show Up Mindfully

Before the day begins, we can remember our own mindfulness practice. It's wonderful to find a group within our work environment to sit with for 10 to 30 minutes each day. We could try doing a heartfulness practice where we send ourselves and our students kind wishes. Finding our own attention, balance, and open heart is imperative before entering the swirl of the day.

When students arrive, we can greet them with direct attention and a sense of care. Endeavor to see each student without putting him or her in a box created by assumptions. As much as possible, remember that the greatest teaching impact comes through relationships—our emotional accessibility and our compassionate presence throughout the day supports the child's ability to learn.

Obstacles Become Opportunities

When teaching mindfulness, it's always good to have a clear plan and be willing to let it go. When obstacles to the plan arise, we can use them as teaching moments. When there are lots of distractions, we can use them as ways to strengthen our attention. When there is a conflict between students, we can explore forgiveness and empathy. If there is stress about an upcoming test, we can scrap the old plan and focus on how wound up the class is so we can start to relax. Whatever comes up during our class can become a part of the lesson. If kids start laughing, if they are annoyed by mindfulness—whatever arises becomes an opportunity to explore.

Be Real

Being real with our students offers them an experience of authenticity. We don't want to lay any drama from home on our students, but naming how we feel in the moment can be an amazing teaching tool. When there is a lot of commotion in the classroom and we notice our own anxiousness, we may say, "Hey class, I'm noticing a lot of commotion right now. I feel a lot of energy in my own body. Let's take a few breaths to check our inner weather patterns."

We can tell the class we are going to take a mindful moment when we need it. We could say, "I need a few breaths right now to help me feel relaxed and focused. You can take a few breaths with me or just give me a moment." When we model taking care of ourselves and being honest with our needs, it makes it acceptable for students to do the same.

Compassion Is the Key

We all have moments when our compassion is tested. When we are teaching we want to hold onto our intention of supporting each student to learn and thrive. However, some students can really push our buttons. Even when we know that they have a very difficult home life or have been diagnosed with a disorder, it can be hard to maintain our compassion sometimes.

We need to set boundaries and not allow certain behaviors, but our intention needs to stay strong in that we are hoping for the best for our students. Maintaining hope and care for students, even when they are acting out and pushing our boundaries, is an amazing practice. With mindfulness practice we can watch our own emotional responses and do our best to be keep our hearts open. We may not accept their behavior, but we always want to accept them as human beings.

Students Are the Experts

So often as teachers we need to know all the answers. In mindfulness the best thing we know is that we don't know. We can never know for sure what we are going to find when we look inside, and we definitely can't be sure what is happening inside our students. Mindfulness is a path of inquiry and insight. We are giving our students the keys to understanding themselves. Like giving the car keys over to a teenager for the first time, this can be an anxiety-provoking experience.

When we can be the learning companions rather than the all-knowing teachers, we are learning collaboratively with our students. Of course we still need to hold the teacher role, but in the mindfulness laboratory we can also be a student with our students.

Invitational Language

When we are teaching mindfulness, we can remember to teach from a place of kindness and presence. One clear way to remember this is to become aware of our language. We wouldn't want to say something like, "Now we are going to be mindful so you have to close your eyes and focus on your breath." We want to make our language more of an invitation rather than an order. We may say, "Now we have an opportunity to learn about being mindful. We can let our eyes close, or just look downward if that feels more comfortable, and we can bring our attention to the breath."

We can't force anyone to do mindfulness. Even if we ordered them to do it, we can't enforce what they do in their own minds. We want to use language that truly gives students a choice about learning to know themselves and their world better.

Optional and Open to Everyone

Mindfulness should always be an option for those who want it and optional for those who don't. When it is optional, students get to own it for themselves. It is far more productive to let a child sit on the side in the beginning and enter later of their own interest than to mandate participation from the beginning and drag them along the whole time.

Mindfulness classes should not be limited to those students who have excelled in class or have "earned" the opportunity. Even if a child is being distracting or difficult, make sure not to exclude them from mindfulness time. Sometimes a class needs to go slowly to bring everyone on board rather than trying to speed up by getting rid of obstacles. Mindfulness is for everyone; if the interest is there, offer it.

Routine

Students are supported by consistency and special routines. This is especially true with a practice like mindfulness, where we are inviting students to enter into stillness and introspection. We can begin and end the session with the ring of a bell, some fun movements, or a song the students like. We demarcate the mindfulness time as one in which there are no tests or grades. It is a space of acceptance and contemplative learning. We can shift the seating arrangement, change the lighting, put a beautiful piece of fabric on the ground for every one to sit on, or any other routine that helps students enter into a mindful state.

It can be beneficial to schedule mindfulness lessons at the same time every day so students can feel consistency. Weaving short mindful moments throughout the day helps reinforce the lessons and deepens the practice. We can schedule moments of mindfulness at particular times during the day where students may need to relax after a transition or build energy and attention late in the day.

Not Another Test

To teach mindfulness, it is important to treat the material differently than a normal lesson. As much as possible, we don't want mindfulness to turn into another subject that students need to be stressed about getting good grades for. We are not giving students information to memorize; we are inviting them to make their own discoveries. When we begin our mindfulness lesson, we can delineate the time by ringing a bell or shifting the seating arrangement. This welcomes the students into a space where they can let down their guard and feel like they do not need to prove anything.

No Wrong Answers

There are no wrong answers within mindfulness. Whatever students experience is perfect. They may say they feel peaceful and happy, or they may say they feel bored or irritated. All of these answers are perfect as long as they are what the student is authentically experiencing. If a student says they think mindfulness is irritating, this is a great opportunity to say, "Thank you for your honesty. I am interested why being quiet and still is so irritating. What happens inside when you are focusing on your breath?" This question very well may open up a great conversation about the difficulty of working with a distracted mind. Instead of a student's comments being a problem, we can engage with them to really learn what is going on in their minds and explain for them the purpose of mindfulness.

Within Range

The pace at which we teach mindfulness is dictated by how fast the class can learn. We need to check our expectations of how fast we want to move and continually return to tracking the capacity of the students. Make sure everyone is on board before the bus pulls away.

We can learn the range of each group of students for how long they feel comfortable sitting in silence. Often students are only able to sit silently for 20 seconds at first; eventually they may be happy practicing for five minutes. The range will even change depending on how kids are feeling at any particular moment. We need to read our students to tell how open they will be to being mindful of their bodies, their chaotic minds, and their emotions. In mindfulness, success is not measured in how far we get but by how connected we are.

Learn from the Class

The best way to learn how to support our students is to observe the dynamics in the class to support the system. If we notice that students generally get distracted and fidgety an hour before lunchtime, then this is great information to keep in mind about when to do some mindful movements. If students seem more relaxed and happy when the seats are arranged in a circle, then we learned which set-up affects their nervous systems best. We can observe our class and experiment with the ways we teach in order to have the best effect.

Agreements

When creating classroom agreements we can explain some of the non-negotiables, such as not harming other students. Then we can ask students what they would like to have as class rules in order to feel more safe and productive. Students may say they don't want kids to be mean to each other, and then there can be some great discussions to see if everyone wants to agree on this. We can have an ongoing list on the wall of our classroom with agreements that can be adapted and updated throughout the year. Students have less resistance to rules when they are a part of creating them, and they learn a priceless skill in community process.

ENGAGING
OUR AUDIENCE

Depending on the age and demographics of our class, we can make mindfulness interesting by introducing it through various themes and popular culture references. We might consider talking about professional sports teams that practice mindfulness, dancers who use their breath to balance, the neuroscience of how mindfulness actually changes the brain, or how mindfulness will help students with reactivity so they can avoid getting into trouble. Here are some engaging examples of how to make mindfulness accessible.

Stories

Students love learning through stories. We can choose books or movies with characters that students resonate with to elucidate points about empathy or attention. We can tell stories about animals or popular figures that embody balance or kindness. Students can be engaged by trying to cultivate the same qualities that the characters are portraying in the story.

Games

We can lead fun games to engage students in attention or kindness practices, which helps them not equate mindfulness with boredom. There are so many great games that use attention, balance, and cooperation. We can play these games and weave in some mindfulness to show how the practices help cultivate the qualities needed for the game.

Art, Music, and Dance

Teaching mindfulness with art, music, and dance helps kids to engage with the practices in a direct and fun way. Some mindfulness teachers have come up with amazing raps and other songs for kids to sing along with and learn mindfulness through music. Other teachers use art practices to reflect on how their students feel inside. There are so many creative ways to help look inside.

Sports

Mindfulness helps players focus, heightens sensory awareness, and supports confidence in play. An amazing amount of athletes now practice mindfulness, including Lebron James, the Seattle Seahawks, and the Women's Olympic gold medal hockey team. Students can practice slow mindful baseball swings or free throws to feel what being present in sports is like.

Neuroscience

Scientific evidence is piling up that shows the way mindfulness builds executive functioning and limits dysregulation, actually changing parts of the brain. We can talk to kids about how mindfulness relaxes the reactive reptilian part of the brain so that the more evolved neocortex can take charge. Students can gain an empowered view of strengthening their focus, impulse control, and other capacities by learning about the ways that mindfulness affects things like the amygdala.

Tests and Grades

We can explain to students how building focus muscles helps us concentrate on the test or lesson at hand so that we excel in school. Instead of needing to read the same page over and over because we keep getting distracted, we can stay focused on our assignments and complete them efficiently with more free time to enjoy when we're done.

Making Friends

For all students, it is important to have friends and get along with peers. Mindfulness can help them increase their friendship skills by practicing active listening, compassion, and authenticity. We can talk to kids about social insecurity and the dramas we get caught up in so easily.

Being Happy

One of the miraculous benefits of mindfulness is that it builds happiness. We all get stuck in the doldrums, but practicing mindfulness can lift us up and put us in a brighter state of mind. It is important for kids to understand that mindfulness isn't just about focusing and working with difficult emotions. When practiced over time, it leads to a happier state of mind and feeling more content with life.

Stressed Out

Students carry their own mixture of stresses. Whatever the stress, we can talk to them about how mindfulness helps us relax, feel better in our bodies, and stay balanced amidst chaos. We can use basic practices such as tightening up and letting go on an exhale to show them how we can use these practices to quickly release tension.

Anger and Reactivity

Everybody has acted or reacted in ways they wish they hadn't at some point. No one likes to get in trouble or be in conflict with others. With mindfulness, students can develop impulse control and anger management skills. We can explain to students how we are giving them the controls to their own emotions with mindfulness so they can choose the way they want to react and feel.

NURTURING
A MINDFUL
CLASSROOM

Researchers have learned that thinking outside the box is not just a cool metaphor but that students literally think better outside of the box. Some students were asked to sit inside a huge cardboard box while others sat right outside of it. When asked word task questions aimed at gauging creativity, the students sitting outside the box scored 20 percent better. Researchers also had them answer questions while some consistently walked on a rectangular path and other students were able to walk freely. The students who were able to walk freely turned out answers that were 25 percent more original (Leung al., 2011).

We want to cultivate conditions where we and our students can thrive. The physical spaces we create for our students can inspire them and regulate their nervous systems. We have the capacity to change the school experience with the lighting we use, the formation of chairs, the schedule, music we play, and other factors.

The following are recommendations for us to create a peaceful, engaging, and fun learning environment. The best way to create a mindful space is to see how the environment affects our own nervous systems. Then we can ask our students questions and track how the different environment affects the classroom. As mindful teachers, we are gardeners with precious seeds.

Shaping the Space

> Shift the seating into a circle or another configuration that is conducive to relaxation and group cohesiveness.

> Create a peaceful atmosphere by changing the lighting. Bright overhead lights are generally overbearing. Get as much natural light as possible.

> Creating a landscape of sound for different moments in the day can be very helpful. Soft ambient music during study times can be inspiring. Upbeat music can also be wonderful in moments where the students need to move their bodies and have a break.

> Create an area within the room that can be a space to relax and regulate. Students can self-refer to this space when they are feeling dysregulated, rather than viewing it as a punishment zone. The area can have art supplies and other soothing things to help them calm down.

> Put up images of inspiring figures or beautiful art and nature. Bring a sense of home and vitality to the classroom with color and art.

> Bring in plants and other natural things. If the class can spend time outside, even better. If not, then bringing in some plants or animals is a great way to connect them with nature.

> Natural scents can be relaxing for students and help create a nice environment. Natural essential oil diffusers are a subtle way to create a nice scent in the room and are generally nonallergenic.

> Stress toys and other nondistracting ways for students to work out some tension in the midst of a lesson are a great addition. Some students need ways to move their bodies and regulate themselves, and we can find ways to help them do this without interrupting others.

> Taking recommendations from students about how they would like the room is important. Ask them what would help them relax and feel inspired. Ask them what in the room isn't working for them.

MINDFUL CLASSROOM WORKSHEET

For this exercise, we can either go to our own classroom or simply imagine the classroom. We will be exploring the space to get a feel for how we can shift it to make it more welcoming and conducive for learning.

MINDFUL CLASSROOM

We can begin by either walking into the room or closing our eyes and envisioning the room. Notice how being in the room feels. Write down how entering the room effects our emotions and general energy.

_____

_____

_____

_____

Spend a few moments imagining how we could completely reshape the space. We can let our fantasies roam to imagine changing the lights, knocking down some walls, and creating the perfect room. What ideas come up?

_____

_____

_____

_____

Take a moment to sit or imagine sitting in some of the student's chairs. Notice what it feels like to take their perspective of the room. Write down any insights that emerge.

_____

_____

_____

_____

Still from the perspective of the students, think of what they may want in order to feel more comfortable and engaged in the classroom. Spend some time in the student's shoes and then write down any ideas.

_____

_____

_____

_____

A DEVELOPMENTAL MINDFULNESS MODEL

Human development from a mindfulness perspective can be seen as a progressive expansion of our circles of awareness, understanding, and compassion. We hope that by instilling stress reduction, resilience, self-compassion, and prosocial behavior, healthy development will be unobstructed. We all have bumps in the road in our upbringing. Because of unmet needs, aspects of development can get arrested and a sense of security in relationships can be compromised. We can't fix the lives of every child, but we can give them tools to help them navigate the obstacles they face as they grow.

The ideal mindful progression is that we begin as children, beautifully egocentric, focused primarily on ourselves. We slowly grow into the world, learning to be compassionate to those around us. As we develop we learn empathy through the capacity to take another's perspective. Then we build the capacity to open our compassion to all of humanity, even those we may judge or dislike. Eventually we open our understanding and reverence for the vast ecological web we are a part of. As in most developmental models, we retain our initial stages as we expand. Our self-compassion stays with us as we learn to be kind to others and eventually gain an awareness of interconnectedness.

The following description of mindfulness practices for different developmental stages is a beginning attempt to understand what will support the growth of compassion and attention at different ages as well as what may be counterindicated. Some practices, such as witnessing thought patterns, may not be developmentally possible for younger students. We need to be strategic with our mindfulness practices to meet the appropriate developmental goals of each age group.

In psychology we often say that we need to build a strong sense of self before we can become selfless. Young children are still developing a solid sense of themselves, and we initially need to help them know themselves before we try more expansive mindfulness practices. Eventually these practices can support students to inquire into their assumptions, judgments, and thought constructs so they can see themselves and the world more clearly. When students have built a healthy sense of self, then they have the ability to open their awareness to a larger worldview and commitment to compassionate action.

Mindfulness Practices for Grades K–2

At this age mindfulness can help students with their self-regulation skills, attention building, and empathy development. Young students learn best through games, stories, and experiential lessons. Socially and academically, kids at this age learn a sense of industry when they can gain skills and prove merit. Impulse control, attention, and empathy can be incredibly empowering as inner skills.

We teach these skills by playing mindfulness. We can teach young children how to feel their breath by having them lie down and place a teddy bear on their bellies to notice how the bear rises and falls with their breathing. We could have students run around, then move in slow motion, and finally freeze completely still. We could have them give each other flowers or other nice things and see what it feels like inside to be generous. Basically we find playful ways to explore mindfulness themes and invite the students to have moments of reflection.

Because the minds of younger children are so plastic, it is that much more important that we create a loving, nonjudgmental, safe space in which they can learn. We support the development of kindness, attention, and emotional regulation in young children, not in a conceptual way but by embodying these factors in the way we teach. Therefore the most important mindfulness practices at this stage are not for the students but for us as teachers.

CONSIDERATIONS

When working with the attention spans of young children, we usually need to offer shorter mindfulness practices—a maximum of a few minutes. Even if we only have students breathing or moving in slow motion for 10 seconds, that is still a good opportunity to be mindful. When offering a full lesson from the curriculum section we will want around fifteen minutes to go through everything.

We want to make sure the classroom feels really safe and comfortable for mindfulness practice, especially with younger students. We may have certain kids sit apart from each other or set up the room in such a way that students will feel the least distracted. At the end of sessions students can reflect on the practices by drawing about certain themes in their mindfulness journal.

RECOMMENDATIONS

> For students at this age, our mindfulness practices are taught mostly through games, stories, and in-the-moment lessons.

> Make the practices embodied. Using fun movements, slow motion, shaking and being still are all great ways to help kids become aware without forcing them to be still.

> Using visuals and props to explain different mindfulness themes helps students be engaged and makes the lessons memorable.

> Telling stories during the lessons helps students resonate with the characteristics of attention and compassion.

> For younger students, it is usually easy for them to be compassionate toward themselves. Having them send kind wishes to themselves is a great way to keep this capacity strong.

> Students may not cognitively understand the goals of the mindfulness practices, but when they are able to experience the benefits the practices can become habitual.

> Building attention for this age group is fun when using distraction games and other ways to explicitly maintain focus.

> Most students at this age love to share what they are experiencing. Give plenty of time for students to share with each other what's going on inside.

Mindfulness for Grades 3-5

Mindfulness eventually supports the difficult realization that we are not the center of the universe. Slowly, through mindful development students, learn to be empathic toward a widening circle of their world. They learn empathy as they build the capacity to see from other perspectives and understand what is asked of them in their schools and communities. We can teach them focusing and emotional regulation practices supporting them in gaining greater skill and autonomy.

With the evolution of self-awareness can come self-criticalness and insecurity. There is a great need to please at this stage, and relationships are extremely important. Social anxiety and performance anxiety can arise at this time in a child's life. Impulse control, calming strategies, and other self-regulation skills become invaluable mindfulness practices.

CONSIDERATIONS

Students at this age are developing a greater capacity to maintain attention. Many can practice silent mindful breathing for 5 or 10 minutes after a few months of working up to it. Even with the greater attention span, we mostly want to engage students through fun and creative lessons.

The full mindfulness lesson can last anywhere from 15 to 30 minutes. Students can appreciate having discussions at this point about the mindfulness themes. They can also enjoy journaling and reflecting on what they learned in the practice.

RECOMMENDATIONS

> At this age executive functioning is developing, giving students higher capacity to reflect and reason. Students can begin to recognize attention as a tool to develop and strengthen.

> Still at this age, the most accessible way to teach kids is through games, stories, and experiential lessons. We want to *play* attention instead of pay attention.

> Talk to students about the benefits of these lessons. At this age they appreciate the rationale behind what they are doing rather than just being told what to do.

> This grade range is when testing begins in some schools, and many other outside stresses start to affect kids. With mindfulness, students can learn to work with their thoughts and stressors in a whole new way.

> Students begin developing more social awareness and capacity for empathy. Using empathy practices, they can build emotional intelligence.

> Students also begin to experience more insecurity. This is a great time to use self-compassion practices.

> Students at this age are highly social, and we can help them navigate the often drama-filled world with practices that encourage them to cultivate social and emotional skills.

Mindfulness for Grades 6–8

As students get older and more mature, we can bring in more practices that help them witness their thoughts and emotions as well as teaching them to understand their world with greater compassion and wisdom. We teach students to notice judgmental thoughts and disturbing emotions, not as fundamental truths but as passing phenomena. Students can expand their compassion and understanding even to people they don't like.

For this age group, mindfulness practices are ideally used to defuse stressors, support inner guidance, and develop impulse control. Adolescents exist in a turbulent world of inner and outer transformation. Their bodies, minds, and social positions are changing dramatically. They begin observing the world and themselves closely, wondering who they are and how they fit in. This can provoke insecurity and anxiety as well as empowerment and insight.

CONSIDERATIONS

Students at this age can maintain attention much better than they could at a younger age, as well as being more capable of communicating abstract thoughts. When we invite students to practice silently, they may be able to sit silently and focus for up to 10 minutes. They also have a greater ability to share what they experienced inside and communicate about the mechanics of their own minds.

In these upper grades, students are often passing from class to class rather than staying in a single classroom. This may make it difficult to spend longer periods of time leading lessons since the class may only be an hour or less. Practices can be led in short, five-minute chunks (or shorter). However, for a full lesson we want 20 minutes to an hour to move through all the steps. We want time for practice as well as for reflection and dialogue.

RECOMMENDATIONS

> Insecurity and self-criticism can be very strong for children at this age. With mindfulness practices, we teach how to witness disturbing thought patterns and not get caught up in them.

> Students can also become very judgmental toward others. We help them be aware of their assumptions and judgments so as not to be mean.

> Bullying can become a serious problem in this age group. Understanding the emotions of self and others is much more possible at this point of cognitive development, and cultivating this understanding may be a very effective way of relieving the pressures of bullying.

> At this point we want to offer students worldly examples, such as professional sports players and musicians practicing mindfulness, so they will be inspired by how the practices can help them.

> Students are getting involved in more complex relational dynamics and truly can use some skills in communication and empathic relating.

> Students also gain a wider lens at this age of seeing how their actions affect the world and how they are affected by the world around them. We can begin teaching practices around global literacy.

> Students now have a great capacity to understand how the brain works. We can teach the benefits of mindfulness on attention, emotional regulation, and executive functioning, with discussions of how this may help them in their lives.

> It is important to remember that at this age, students may begin having a lot of insecurity around their bodies, gender, and other senses of socially fitting in. We can teach self-compassion and develop a safe class to communicate within.

Mindfulness for Grades 9–12

Teenagers have families, friends, teachers, media, and a host of other influences pulling them in different directions. They seek to recognize their own individual identity, having grown out of childhood, and they are constructing their own path. Underneath all the coolness and insecurity there is the deep question of "Who am I?" Teenagers want to fit in, but they also want to be authentic. They want to know how to be liked, while simultaneously wanting to be themselves and not fake it.

Mindfulness offers teenagers a way to connect to a deeper authenticity and inner compass. It also offers a more skillful way of interacting with others. Cognitively, mindfulness can help them gain a greater understanding of cause and effect, witnessing how their behaviors affect others and how they want to be treated. Exploring how their minds, hearts, and bodies are affected by the world helps them understand how their actions and thoughts affect others. This is the age at which mindfulness practices can be used for service projects and to actively bring compassion into the world.

CONSIDERATIONS

Teenagers have the ability to really take the mindfulness practices as their own, using the time to relax and develop self-awareness. They can practice silently for 10 minutes or longer. For an extended lesson students need from 30 minutes to an hour. Much of the time can be spent in dialogue discussing how the practices can support them.

Since most high school students move from classroom to classroom, teachers will need to find a way to introduce moments of practice into classes. It can be best to have extracurricular mindfulness clubs, where the students really have time to communicate and explore the practices. There are even weeklong mindfulness retreats led for teenagers where they practice long silent sittings. Even in short practices, though, mindfulness lessons can be very supportive for students experiencing the stress of the teen years. Practices can be used before tests, in conflict management, and in other difficult situations. Mindfulness journals can become a reflection exercise that supports inner exploration.

RECOMMENDATIONS

> At this age we really want to help students own these practices. Teenagers need to experience mindfulness practice as a personal project or it will be yet another thing they feel is forced on them.

> Students can be inspired by the idea of gaining mastery of these practices so that they can succeed in sports, social relations, and other situations that are exciting for them.

> Life for teens is very peer-centered. It is important to weave in social components to make the training more engaging. We show students how these practices support self-esteem and strengthen social skills.

> Share with students how kindness is sometimes seen as uncool by teenagers, but that deep down everyone wants to be liked and have friends. We help students see how cool being kind and compassionate is.

> Empowering students to take their mindfulness practice into the world with service projects and kind acts is a wonderful way to engage them.

> We can begin showing students how their assumptions turn into biases and how important it is to be introspective to make the world a more empathic place.

> Teens extend their understanding and compassion into the larger world to see the interconnectedness to other cultures and the larger ecology. We help open their world views and inspire them to be active in their choices.

> We can help students to look inside and realize which qualities, such as kindness, emotional regulation, or attention, they want to focus on and develop.

DEVELOPMENTAL MINDFULNESS WORKSHEET

As adults we still have our own inner child parts. We may still have rebellious teen parts, insecure middle school parts, and scared kindergarten parts. Often our corresponding kid parts come out when we are with different age groups. We may feel our insecure parts when talking in front of a group of adolescents or our exuberant or scared little kid parts when we are in an elementary school classroom. With mindfulness this is not seen as a problem. In fact, we can use this strange phenomenon as a way to empathically attune to the youth we are with. In this worksheet we can gain some understanding of the developmental stages our students are going through and gain empathy for them by getting in touch with what it was like when we were that age.

DEVELOPMENTAL MINDFULNESS

What are the ages and developmental stages of the youth you are working with?

_____

_____

_____

What developmental themes are you tracking in your students right now?

_____

_____

_____

What was your school experience like when you were this age?

_____

_____

_____

What was most important to you in your life at this age?

_____

_____

_____

What were your biggest stressors and struggles at this time?

_____

_____

_____

What people and experiences were supportive in your development in this time?

_____

_____

_____

What social and emotional support do you wish you had received at this time?

_____

_____

_____

In what ways can you empathize with your students' developmental struggles?

_____

_____

_____

What role would you like to play in supporting the development of your students?

_____

_____

_____

How do you hope mindfulness will support your students in their particular development?

_____

_____

_____

DIVERSITY AND QUESTIONING ASSUMPTIONS

We all have assumptions and biases. Our minds are built that way to learn from past experiences and keep us safe in the future. The problem is that a lot of those assumptions are not actually true, and they tend to alienate us from others. Maybe our parents warned us about certain types of people because they wanted to keep us safe. The problem is that any time we take a whole group—such as people with tattoos, homeless people, or certain races—and attach an assumption, we have dehumanized the whole group. When we lay assumptions on our students, they are no longer human beings with whole worlds inside them and great hopes for their futures. They just become an Indian kid, or a black kid, or a Latino kid, or any other category that we place on them. En masse these assumptions become bullying, segregation, and oppression.

When assumptions are left unchecked, we find ourselves in a culture with great socioeconomic and racial disparity. The Department of Education has found in schools around the United States, students of color are suspended three times as often as white students and get less access to veteran teachers (US Department of Education, 2014). When psychologists have plumbed the depth of this inequality, their research has shown that adults unconsciously assume black children are less innocent than their white peers (Goff et al., 2014). With the heartbreaking inequality in our schools, we need a great systemic shift. To make that shift, we need to begin by inquiring into our own hearts and minds.

Even as well-intentioned mindful educators, we are at risk of teaching mindfulness in such a way that is laden with assumptions and without cultural competency. In schools with high levels of stress, teachers may want to bring in mindfulness to help students be more calm and attentive. The problem with this is that classrooms with extremely dysregulated students are struggling for a reason. Instead of just trying to get them to sit still and listen, we first want to understand the difficulties they face. Is there systemic inequality? Are students facing ongoing trauma? Are there some basic human needs to tend before we get into mindfulness teaching? We need to be aware of the socioeconomic experience of our students before we teach them mindfulness.

The good news is that by using our mindful attention and compassion skills, we can begin the inner shift that hopefully will help create greater equity in our world. One study showed that practicing mindfulness actually limited racial bias. Participants who practiced mindfulness relied less on previously held assumptions and were therefore less biased toward different races (Lueke and Gibson, 2014). In another study on implicit bias, they found that when Caucasian research participants practiced compassion meditation, their bias toward African Americans and homeless people decreased (Kang et al., 2014). As educators we can learn this capacity to open our minds and see the world through a lens of compassion.

In the curriculum section if this book, we explore teaching social literacy to students. Here we try to build our own social and cultural literacy by looking at our own biases to widen our perspectives. Our authentic exploration of the assumptions we hold will help us know ourselves better and therefore see our students more clearly. Then we can be role models for all of our students, regardless of their race or gender, as people willing to ask questions about inequality. Questioning our assumptions isn't something we do once and then we are off the hook. We can live our whole lives looking at where there is inequality around us and uncovering our blind spots. This is mindfulness in action.

How to Question Our Own Assumptions

Caring About Inequality: When we look into the world we can see how some are born into privilege and others into poverty. We can simply bring our awareness to this fact without any ideas of whose fault it is or how we are going to fix it. The first step is facing the hard truth of inequality, knowing the suffering it causes, and feeling hope for healing.

Turning In: Next we need to turn inward and realize that we all have assumptions and uncovering them will bring less bias into the world. It takes bravery for us to look inward and root out assumptions and biases. We can explore our habitual assumptions toward gender, different races, people of different sexual orientations, or any other group of people we may think of as other.

Thought Spotting: Next we look at our assumptions pertaining to these groups. What thoughts are connected to them? Do we think one group is smarter, another more violent, another cooler? Just observe what we think we know about these big groups of people.

Noting Emotions: Then we look into our feelings about each group. Imagine they are walking down the street toward us. Do we feel scared, happy, disgusted, excited? Without any judgment for ourselves, we can notice how we emotionally respond to each of these groups.

Know We Don't Know: Once we have noticed our thoughts and feelings, we can question their validity. We can admit that these are just theories and feelings and see if we can watch them floating by like our breath. This can be uncomfortable to do, so as we witness our assumptions we can just feel what it's like not to attach ourselves to our judgments.

Learning About Our World: Once we pull people out of the boxes we had put them in, we get to have some fun. Look around at all the people we thought we knew and meet them anew. We might get interested in different cultures and ways of seeing the world. Instead of difference being scary, it can become exciting and fascinating.

Discernment: Of course we don't want to completely let go of assumptions. If a dangerous-looking person is walking toward us, we need to rely on some assumptions and discern whether we are being biased or if this is actually a threat. We want to keep the door open to each new experience, but we want to keep a bouncer there to discern who gets in.

We can use our mindfulness practice to open our eyes to systemic injustice and notice what it feels like in our hearts to witness such socioeconomic discrepancies. The appropriate response to injustice is often sadness and anger. We want to be able to see the problems, feel their impact, and fight for what's right. We hope to be able to bring the empowering practices of mindfulness to support all those in need with emotional regulation, inner resilience, and open heartedness. More and more we want to offer the strengths of mindfulness to the social justice movement and learn the wisdom of diversity and inclusion from so many who have fought tirelessly for their rights. We need to be mindful with social justice in mind.

TRAUMA-INFORMED TEACHING

As teachers, we encounter students with many forms and levels of stress and trauma. There is big "T" trauma; the type of disturbance that results from sexual abuse, violent conflicts, and other forms of severe mistreatment. There are also the little "t" traumas that we all carry with us. Maybe we were bitten by a dog, were picked on in school, or just had an argument with a friend. Trauma means that we have had a disturbing experience that was too much for our emotional system to process. Therefore the experience remains unresolved, carried around in the body, the past experience affecting and distorting the way we respond to the present moment.

Simply put, mindfulness and trauma are opposites. Mindfulness means being embodied in the present moment, bringing our attention to our emotions, sensations, relationships, and our ever-transforming experience. Trauma, on the other hand, is the protective mechanism that distances us from the present moment, dissociates us from our bodies, and turns us away from our emotions and difficult sensations. Trauma occurs when a distressing experience or an ongoing difficulty is so great that we lose our capacity to adequately respond. With trauma, our inner sentry is always on high alert, as if the initial trauma is still physically imminent, even if the current situation is completely safe.

Growing up in a neighborhood where a child is perpetually scared for their lives, hearing gunshots at night, and having multiple family members who have been incarcerated will often lead to what is called complex post-traumatic stress disorder. There doesn't need to be a particular incident of trauma; if the generalized life experience is one of fear, the child will learn to engage with the world as an unsafe place, even if the circumstances change. Becoming aware of the high alert that some students' nervous systems operate on helps us understand and support them.

Research on trauma, neglect, and abuse have given us a window into their tragic effects on the brain, genetics, and patterns that those suffering from them develop over a lifetime. The Adverse Childhood Experience (ACE) study has shown how difficult early childhood experiences set a path for obesity, drug use, criminality, and other behaviors correlated with stress. "The ACE Study also showed that as the ACE score increased the number of risk factors for the leading causes of death increased. Thus, persons with high ACE scores are later at much higher risk for health and medical conditions resulting from their choice of remedies for their pain. While these approaches are effective in the short term, they often have dire long-term consequences such as serious chronic health and social problems" (Felliti et al., 1998).

A privileged school can be a traumatizing environment as well. If the high-stakes testing and pressure to succeed is great enough, the stress can become so unbearable that students develop anxiety and depression. Even in some of the most affluent communities, the suicide rates for teens are staggering. Many adults report still having terrifying dreams of not having studied for a big test or realizing they are naked in the classroom much later in life. Obviously if we are still having anxious school dreams in our forties, the stress must have made some very real residual impacts.

Trauma itself is a division from the present moment, so mindfulness is a possible antidote to invite kids back into their bodies. It is also imperative to help kids find a place where they feel safe. Some trauma trainings work on helping people find a safe space they can return to in their minds whenever they get too afraid in their bodies. With mindfulness we are cultivating an inner state of stillness, safety, and happiness. Creating this base of safety may give kids who have had trauma or continue to live in traumatic situations a refuge.

The hope is that mindfulness can intervene to relax the inner sentry and bring the nervous system back to a balanced state. With the integrative effects that mindfulness has on the brain, the hope would be that the inevitable stressors of life will not get caught in the body in the first place. It has been shown how two people can share the same dramatic experience but respond to it very differently—one with trauma, the other with a harrowing story that can become empowering. The determining factor seems to be whether the person had the inner skills to meet the experience with resilience and hope rather than hopelessness and shame.

Creating a base of safety to which kids can return when they notice that they are dysregulated helps them build resilience—the capacity to be with difficult experiences and rise above adversity. Being able to tolerate difficulties allows us to be present in the midst of harsh conditions and not shut down or disassociate. Mindfulness supports in the process of staying present and holding ourselves in compassion, not blaming ourselves or suppressing our feelings.

In many cutting-edge trauma psychology modalities, practitioners use basic mindfulness practices to help mediate trauma and stressful experiences. Psychologists invite patients to feel their feet on the ground, name the colors on the walls in the room, and use other ways to orient the client into the present moment experience. Teaching students to return attention to present-moment sensory experiences helps them build a base of safety in the present moment, which they can shift back to when they are caught in ruminating thoughts or traumatic memories.

Embodied mindfulness can integrate a stressed system, but we need to be aware that mindfulness practices can also provoke difficult emotional responses in children that, without adequate containment, can have adverse affects. Usually kids learn to build emotional armoring, and when a mindfulness class opens a safe and caring atmosphere, these locked-in emotions may spring forth. We want students to have a safe space to bring their full emotional experience, but if the container is not adequately held, the release will be a retraumatization rather than a corrective experience.

There is profound healing possible through mindfulness, but we need to be aware of the mechanism of trauma and the effects of different mindfulness practices. Without adequate understanding of trauma, a mindfulness teacher could unwittingly push a student into a sensory awareness that was overly distressing. There is a danger of mindfulness becoming a dissociative practice rather than an embodied and healing one.

To mitigate these dangers, we need to study trauma and stress-related disorders. Not only can we become sensitive and skilled with our students, we can learn how to care for our own stress and trauma. We all have vicarious stress and trauma from teaching, as well as the scrapes and bruises we collected on our own journeys to adulthood. In expanding the capacity to care for ourselves, our hearts stretch open and gain the emotional navigation skills to support students in the landscape of their own hearts.

Mindful Pointers

> It is important to remember that mindfulness—emotional practices in particular—can stimulate difficult responses in children. Develop a strong network of collateral resources, such as school therapists, social workers, and local agencies. We can use these resources to consult with and refer students to if they reveal trauma or abuse.

> If we have abuse or trauma in our own history, it can be very healing to seek out therapy or trauma support, such as Eye Movement Desensitization and Reprocessing (EMDR), Somatic Experiencing, or Hakomi. Not only can this help in transforming our own trauma, it can help in understanding how to be of support to our students.

> It is very important to understand the stressors and traumas of the students that we work with. Learn about students' communities, families, and local environments to gain a greater understanding of their stressors, as well as their resources.

> Kids need to know what to do with toxic stress. If they are not given adequate practices and venues to relieve their tensions, the basic physics of the body necessitates some other form of release. If they don't have a healthy way, kids are apt to choose the endless unhealthy opportunities at their disposal.

TRAUMA-INFORMED TEACHING WORKSHEET

Take a moment to answer the following questions about stressors you imagine your students may have. When we know about the possible stressors and traumas in our students' lives, it is easier to cultivate empathy and understanding for their behaviors. Instead of just being frustrated by the students who are dysregulated and distracting everyone else, we can learn about what these students are struggling with and how we can help.

TRAUMA-INFORMED TEACHING

What are some basic human needs your students may not be getting met?

_____
_____
_____
_____

What are some of the particular stressors your students face because of the community they live in?

_____
_____
_____
_____

What stressors may your students face because of their race, class, or gender?

_____
_____
_____
_____

What stressors do your students face at their particular age?

_____
_____
_____
_____

What academic stressors do your students face?

_____
_____
_____
_____

What family stressors are some of your students facing?

_____

_____

_____

_____

In what ways are your students' stressors affecting their social, emotional, and academic capacities?

_____

_____

_____

_____

In what ways do you imagine mindfulness could help your students with these stressors?

_____

_____

_____

_____

In what ways could you be more mindful of your students' stressors?

_____

_____

_____

_____

PART I

Mindfulness Lessons for Students

Classroom Activities, Practices, and Techniques

"Each morning, we sit quietly and pay attention to what's going on right in this moment. Through guided practice, we notice our breath, thoughts, physical sensations, emotions, and sounds. We practice sitting quietly and still. I encourage students to notice how their bodies feel as we settle in. This is our routine every morning so the first-graders have come to expect it and look forward to it."
—JENNIFER HARVEY, FIRST-GRADE TEACHER, CALIFORNIA

Now that we know how to embody mindfulness and to set up a mindful space, we can begin teaching these practices to students. Before we teach, we want to remember always to be a student of mindfulness ourselves. The personal development never ends. We need to find balance again and again as the waves of demands and dramas are splashing around us. Instead of this being problematic, we can become surfers of the shifting tides. As we are more mindfully literate, we invariably expand our capacity to read and navigate what's happening inside ourselves and with the dynamics in the class.

We begin this chapter by exploring mindful learning objectives. Before we teach we want to examine the proven positive attributes these practices develop so we can strategically use them for our particular students. Then we look at the mindful lesson layout. We discuss how to deliver mindfulness practices so they are engaging, thought provoking, and assimilated into the daily lives of students. Then we show how to introduce mindfulness to students. We want to be able to present it in such a way that the students don't feel coerced. On the contrary, we want them to feel invited into a fascinating and fun world of self-discovery.

Finally we explore the five literacies of mindful learning. We begin with physical literacy, teaching students the language of their bodies to develop awareness, relaxation, and well-being. Then we advance to mental literacy, helping students learn about attention, distraction, thoughts, metacognition, and the mechanics of their minds. We proceed to emotional literacy, supporting students in learning how to regulate difficult emotions and foster emotions such as happiness, gratitude, and compassion. Then we introduce social literacy, empowering students to bring their attention and compassion into relationships and cultural contexts. Next we teach global literacy, expanding their mindful lenses to understand and care for the world all around them. Finally we explore integration practices from which we can weave mindfulness into the fabric of our school days.

As we study these lessons, it is important to consider how mindfulness-based curriculum is a bit of an oxymoron. As we have been learning, mindfulness is about being present and empathically responsive to our ever-shifting world. Creating a step-by-step model for teaching will always be somewhat reductive. Every class is different, and the classroom atmosphere changes depending on the time of day and a million other factors. This curriculum should be treated less like a linear model to be followed to the letter and more like a toolbox to build a mindful classroom in collaboration with students.

MINDFUL LEARNING OBJECTIVES

The following learning objectives have been drawn from mindfulness research. Throughout the curriculum section, each lesson will have a list of these learning objectives that the particular practice aims to support. There is a profusion of mindfulness research that has been building for the past 30 years in medicine, neuroscience, and psychology. In the past 10 years the young field of mindfulness in education has begun to publish an array of promising research. Use this list of learning objectives as a starting point to explain the benefits of mindfulness to students and the school community.

Executive Functioning

Mindfulness practices work to return students from distraction and dysregulation to a sustained point of focus, building a capacity to witness and regulate with executive functioning. *Executive functioning* refers to the internal system that controls and regulates our cognitive processes. To solve problems and think critically, students need to strengthen this essential cognitive capacity. Mindfulness practice has been found to benefit executive functioning in elementary age students, especially those who begin with executive functioning impairment (Flook et al., 2010). Neuroscience researchers have found that brief regular mindfulness practices can improve executive functioning and its neurobiological mechanisms (Tang et al., 2012).

Emotional Self-Regulation

Students can learn with these lessons a direct way to witness their dysregulation, track their emotions, and bring themselves back to equilibrium. We need to regulate our emotions to be ready to learn. Difficult emotions have the capacity to hijack our educational capacity and the direction of our lives. Researchers have found that mindfulness helps strengthen the parts of the brain correlated with emotional regulation, such as the prefrontal cortex, while down-regulating the parts of the brain associated with emotional processing, such as the amygdala (Lutz et al., 2014). Researchers found that high school students receiving mindfulness training improved their emotional regulation capacity, self-reporting greater emotional awareness, access to regulation strategies, and emotional clarity (Metz et al., 2013).

Metacognition

These lessons offer students the ability to gain objectivity around their thoughts and the phenomenon they experience without being swept up in them. Self-awareness is an innate human capacity, and a mindfulness practice supports our ability to witness our minds, bodies, hearts, and environments. This offers students a greater ability to know when they are dysregulated or when they are distracted and then course correct midstream. Mindfulness-based therapeutic models have proved just as effective with depression relapses as antidepressants. A major aspect of the therapeutic benefits of mindfulness is metacognition's capacity to witness thoughts and emotions without getting flooded by them (Teasdale, 1999). Educational researchers have learned that metacognition is a major factor for students in motivation and self-regulated learning (Efklides, 2011).

Focused Attention

Students build their attention muscles through sustained focus and ability to work with mind wandering and distractions. Attention is a foundation of success for any endeavor. When students are distracted, they usually distract others as well, and much teaching time is spent trying to herd the attention back to the subject at hand. Short attention training practices, repeated regularly, can make amazing differences in the classroom as well as for the long-term focus capacity of students. Long-term mindfulness practitioners actually shift the attentional networks of their brains. Not only do they pay attention better, they are less distracted and disturbed by external stimuli (Brefczynski-Lewis et al., 2007).

In a study where 9–13-year-olds were offered mindfulness-based cognitive therapy, they exhibited fewer attentional problems, which also limited behavioral problems (Semple et al., 2010).

Empathy

In nursery school and kindergarten, teachers spend a lot of time trying to teach kids how to be empathic. Sadly, bullying and student conflicts are still serious problems in most schools. Every student knows that they are "supposed" to be nice to each other, but simply saying this does not have much of an impact. Teaching kindness, compassion, and empathy through mindfulness practices offers a direct experience of opening hearts to others and strengthens empathy and prosocial behavior. In a social-emotional learning program using mindfulness, it was found that students were more empathic and less aggressive and had greater peer acceptance (Schonert-Reichl et al., 2015). Studies have shown that mindfulness practice with adults heightens key empathy-related brain circuitry (Lutz et al., 2008).

Stress Reduction

Stress can disturb students' mental, emotional, and physical balance, disrupting their capacity to learn and socialize. These practices aim at reducing stress and bringing the students back into a physiological homeostasis. Stress makes people less able to hold memories, focus, and be happy. The stress of grades and family life are so high for some kids that they develop serious physical and emotional problems. Relaxation is the key to being able to let go of stress and find balance.

Meta-analysis of the effects of stress on children's brain development has shown how negatively the prefrontal cortex is affected, impairing executive functioning and other cognitive abilities (Hanson et al., 2011). In a review of mindfulness in education research, a key finding throughout schools and youth programs has been the resilience to stress (Zenner et al., 2014).

Self-Compassion

Kindness, compassion, and esteem for ourselves are key ingredients to being healthy and happy. To have genuine esteem and compassion for others, we begin by generating kindness toward ourselves. Self-compassion is a growing field of mindfulness in which we cultivate compassion for our own minds, hearts, and bodies. Self-critical thought patterns, body issues, and emotional disorders are on the rise with youth, and these disturbances are severe hindrances to academic and social-emotional growth. When researchers offered a mindfulness training to adolescents in an outpatient psychiatric facility, they found the students' anxiety, depression, and somatic distress decreased while their self-esteem rose (Biegel et al., 2009). Researchers studied adolescents in a mindfulness-based self-compassion trainings and found that students gained not only greater self-acceptance but also a greater sense of well-being (Neff and McGehee, 2010).

Open-Mindedness

Open-mindedness stimulates the capacity to understand other perspectives and value diversity. Mindfulness offers us the capacity to witness our thoughts and beliefs and gives us the ability to see beyond the narrow lens of our individual perspectives. Instead of getting a fixed mind-set, we develop an adaptive growth mind-set and are open to many perspectives. Studies have found when students practice mindfulness, they are less selfish and exhibit greater prosocial behaviors and social competency (Flook et al., 2015). It also turns out that when we practice open-monitoring meditations, our creativity and insightful problem-solving capacity expands (Colzato et al., 2012).

Contentment

As much as possible, these lessons are meant to be presented in a fun way that helps kids feel good in their bodies. Research shows that we are happier when our minds are not wandering and we are focused in the present moment (Killingsworth and Gilbert, 2010). Wonderfully, an effect of mindfulness practice is the flowering of happiness and contentment. When youth feel safe and cared for, they naturally are playful, creative, and curious about learning. Mindfulness can support students in feeling more relaxed and secure, freeing them up to be happier. A happier student population makes for easier learning and teaching. Studies find that students practicing mindfulness are more calm, relaxed, and have greater self-acceptance (Broderick and Metz, 2009).

Cognitive Flexibility

Mindfulness can support students in making constructive and conscious choices. Meditative practices have been found to support cognitive flexibility, the capacity to shift between different concepts and to hold multiple concepts simultaneously (Moore and Malinowski, 2009). Students learn that they do not need to be at the whim of their thoughts and emotions but can shift awareness and choose where to place attention. Ethical choices are always an option, and students with impulse control and cognitive flexibility can decide how they wish to proceed. Researchers even find that meditative practices help us not get caught in rigid mind-sets and create more flexible and creative brains (Greenberg et al., 2012).

Resilience

These lessons help students be present to difficult emotions and find regulation amidst adversity. Resilience is the capacity to face adversity and struggles and move through them with hope and courage. We all face obstacles, and resilience is the capacity to rise and be strengthened by the difficulty rather than bowing under the weight of the struggle. This endurance to move through difficult times takes determination and perseverance. Some educators call this capacity "grit" and have shown the amazing academic benefits that grit offers those who have developed it. In a mindfulness training, adolescents with conduct disorder were able to develop greater awareness and regulation of their aggressive behavior (Singh et al., 2007). With a mindfulness-based kindness curriculum, researchers found that preschoolers were able to develop greater self-regulatory resilience skills (Flook et al., 2015).

MINDFULNESS LESSON LAYOUT

When introducing new lessons, it is helpful to open up an extended period of time for exploring the themes and practices. It is helpful to spend 15 minutes introducing a new lesson to elementary-age students. For middle and high school students, it can be helpful to spend anywhere from 15 minutes to an hour introducing the practices and discussing. With any group, we want enough time to introduce the new lesson, do the practice, and end with some reflection and integration. The basic flow, as outlined below, works well for students of all age groups. Once the lesson has been introduced, we can reinforce the skills by offering the practices in short form throughout the day, weaving moments of mindfulness into the daily schedule.

> Opening mindful moment
> Check-in and report back
> New lesson introduction
> Experiential practice
> Sharing/dialogue
> Integration/journaling
> Mindful life practice
> Closing mindful moment

Opening Mindful Moment

At the beginning of every mindfulness class, we can start with a mindful moment. If the students have learned a few exercises already, we can start by practicing what we learned in the previous lesson. We can ring a bell to communicate that the class has begun and that everyone can practice for a few minutes. Some of the go-to opening lessons are mindful listening, the anchor breath, and mindful movements. Once students have been practicing mindfulness for some time, we can ask a student to choose and lead the opening practice.

Check-In and Report Back

Once the students have experienced some mindfulness lessons, we can ask them about the ways they have been using their practice in everyday life. At the end of every class we can offer home study assignments in which students are invited to notice their emotions, observe their attention, or engage in other practices related to specific themes. This check-in time helps students begin to understand how they have started using their mindfulness skills in their everyday lives. As they report back on their findings, the whole class can learn and the students can witness their growth in a very satisfying way.

New Lesson Introduction

After the check-in we can introduce the lesson of the day. It is important to remember not to tell the students what they are supposed to experience, but simply set up the lesson as an exploration. If we are presenting Popcorn Thoughts, for instance, we can talk about how students will be given an opportunity to gain greater awareness of the way their minds work and then offer instructions on the practice. We can introduce the theme of the lesson, such as "distraction" or "assumptions." We could give some real-life examples of how we all experience these phenomena. We may even share a story or anecdote that exemplifies this theme to spur interest.

Experiential Practice

After describing the next lesson, it is time to dive into the experiential practice. As always we want to remember to keep it within the range of our students' capacities. We may only spend 30 seconds practicing, or if they are able, we could silently watch our breath for 5 minutes. Here we are inviting students into an exploration and guiding them into the different realms of mindful literacy. Our goal is to give the students a taste of what it's like to experience each lesson theme in a deeply personal and empowering way. If we are practicing with difficult emotions, for example, we want students to get a direct experience of what these emotions feel like in the body and how to self-regulate.

Sharing/Dialogue

It's always helpful to give students some time to share how the experience of the day's practice unfolded for them. By listening openly without judgment, we can learn a lot about each other. Remind the students to share their direct experience without getting lost in stories or ideas about why certain feelings arose. Students can share their experiences in a dialogue, small group discussion, or other forms of mindful communication.

If there is time, it's great to share a story, quote, or exercise that pertains to the topic of the day. For example, if the lesson involved working with difficult emotions, we can share the quote, "You can't stop the waves, but you can learn how to surf." Then we can go around the room and hear students' thoughts about the quote.

Integration/Journaling

It's helpful to give students time to reflect on the lesson in their journals. Younger students can draw pictures, and older students can write down some reflections. If we are doing a gratitude lesson, for example, we might have them draw a picture or write about the things they are grateful for in their lives. These practices help students integrate and make meaning of whatever lesson they have just experienced. This is also a great moment to get creative and see how we can integrate the practices into our particular classroom. Maybe we have students open their books and read a page with their new mindful eyes after a focusing lesson, or we could have them walk around and say kind things to each other after an empathy lesson. We are trying to teach students how to bring the practices into their lives.

Mindful Life Practice

At the end of every lesson, we can suggest a way to explore the theme at hand in daily life. For example, after the mindful movement lesson, we may ask students to notice the sensations in their bodies when they are running on the playground or as they brush their teeth at home. It's great to tell them that there is no homework in mindfulness, and that this is simply an invitation to become mindful investigators in their own lives. Then they can bring back their findings to the next class.

Closing Mindful Moment

At the end of the session, we can again lead a short mindfulness practice. This may only involve a few mindful movements or a minute of belly breathing. Sometimes a mindfulness class will bring students to a very open state, and we want to be sure that transitions are not too abrupt. Let them know that they will be transitioning but that they can stay connected to their attention, their bodies, and their hearts.

INTRODUCING MINDFULNESS TO STUDENTS

When we first teach mindfulness to students, we want to do it in such a way that students feel invited rather than forced. The following steps are recommendations of how to introduce mindfulness so that they feel engaged and welcomed. This may be a new concept for students. When welcoming students to this new way of being in the world, we want to make sure to model mindfulness in the way we present it.

What Is Mindfulness?

Before launching into our own definition of mindfulness, ask the group if they have ever heard of it and what they have heard. We may get some rather profound responses as well as some imprecise assumptions that it will be helpful to clear up. If we start with our own definition of mindfulness, students may simply parrot back to us what they think we want them to say. We can tell the students at first that we will be taking the opportunity to learn about our bodies, our minds, our hearts, and the world around us.

Mindful Moment

We can ask students to simply take a moment and see what they notice. This moment can last anywhere from five seconds to a minute—however long seems to be in range for the students. We don't want to freak them out; we just want to give them a taste of what it is like to be together in a silent and observant space. Usually children will mention that they noticed the stillness that arose when they were being mindful. They may even mention that they noticed new sounds, sensations, or aspects of their minds.

Harvesting Insights

Almost always when we ask students what they notice, we get amazing responses such as, "It got so quiet in here I could hear the buzz of the electric light," or "I noticed how many thoughts are in my head." It's best when we can form a definition of mindfulness by reflecting on the responses with students. We could say, "Wow, it sounds like just by sitting still for a moment you were able to be aware of so many things you otherwise wouldn't have noticed. Mindfulness must make us more aware." We also want to make a wide definition of mindfulness. If students say they feel bored or irritated by mindfulness, we can say, "When we slow down, we notice so many things going on inside and all around us. Mindfulness is about being aware of everything."

How Can We Be More Aware

Once students are getting the idea that mindfulness is about being more aware, we can ask them, "What do you think we could do to be even more aware?" Students will often say things like closing their eyes, being really still, not making any noises, or focusing really hard. It's wonderful when students can give us the strategies instead of us just telling them what to do.

Let's Try That Again

Now invite students to take another mindful moment. This time, they can try to be as still as possible, avoid making any noises, and close their eyes. When we invite youth to close their eyes, we need to remember that for some of them this may not feel safe. We can simply ask these students to focus their gaze on the floor or desk in front of them. We can explain that these practices help us look inside of ourselves, so it is helpful not to get distracted by looking around. For this short moment of mindfulness, invite students to really focus and see what they notice when everything is still and quiet. After this mindful moment, ask again what students noticed.

Safe Space

After our mindful moments, we can explain how mindfulness is an opportunity to look inside ourselves and that we want to create a space where it feels safe to share and be real. To create a safe space, we can ask for some group agreements. We may ask students to agree not to distract each other. It is also important to ask them not to share anything their peers have said in class with anyone outside of the classroom. Once we have explained to students what we would like them to agree to, we can ask them what they think would be helpful to do as a class to help everyone feel more safe and focused. The class can come up with collective agreements on how to make the safest space and discuss them.

THE FIVE REALMS OF MINDFUL LITERACY

We now venture through the five realms of mindful literacy. The physical, mental, emotional, social, and global are realms in which we all need to be fluent to thrive. In each section we find five lessons to explore with our students. It is not necessary to follow the sequence of 25 lessons exactly, although it is important to recognize how certain mindfulness capacities are developed best through progressive stages. Then we have five more integration practices so that we can learn how to use our mindful literacy throughout the day.

As we move through the curriculum, it will become clear why the lessons are ordered how they are. We begin with physical literacy so students can be present and regulated in their bodies. We also want them to learn the language of their bodies because this inner somatic understanding is foundational for future lessons. Then we can move to mental literacy where we are teaching students about witnessing their thoughts and developing focusing skills.

Once we have taught students about the language of the body and the mechanics of mind, we can teach them emotional literacy. We teach students how to watch when they are having judgmental or self-critical thoughts and notice the correlated uncomfortable emotions in the body. When students can track their thoughts and then bring compassion to the difficult emotions in their bodies, we are teaching them impulse control and self-regulation. We would not be able to offer these transformative emotional literacy practices without first teaching the physical and mental capacities of witnessing thoughts and noticing sensations.

Once students have developed capacities such as attention, compassion, and emotional regulation, they can bring them into the world. We are not practicing mindfulness in a vacuum. We help students cultivate these profound qualities so they can communicate compassionately and develop cultural competency. Kids can also become mindful of the global realm in which they depend for every breath and every meal. They can notice the impact they have on other people and their environment, learning to take responsibility and to develop integrity.

Physical Literacy

We hope that our students' stress levels will fall and physical awareness will rise, but how often do we teach them how to create these changes? Before their bodies feel safe, it is incredibly hard for students to pay attention and learn, which is why we begin our lessons with our awareness centered on the body: relaxing, grounding, and having fun. We want to meet kids where they are and help them be present in the room. Through this grounding practice, students can gain a language for expressing what is happening inside their bodies that will help them in later lessons on attention, impulse control, and emotional regulation. We can help students settle their nervous systems, regulate their energy, and cultivate health and well-being.

Mental Literacy

We hope that our students will be able to pay attention and tune out distractions, but how often do we teach them how to do this? Focusing is imperative for academic and extracurricular achievement. Once students are grounded and ready to learn, they can look inside and develop their attention muscles. With mindfulness, students build their attention, work with distraction, and learn to witness their thought patterns. Thought watching is a necessity for impulse control, emotional regulation, and awareness of limiting beliefs and assumptions.

Emotional Literacy

We hope that our students will be happy and able to regulate difficult emotions, but how often do we teach them how to achieve this state of being? Emotional literacy teaches students to work with difficult emotions and strengthen healthy emotional states. We can teach them through practices of embodiment and focus to gain a deep level of sensitivity and awareness of how they are affected by their emotions and how to respond constructively. With mindfulness, emotions become an ally rather than an enemy.

Social Literacy

We hope that our students will be kind and refrain from judging others, but how can we teach them how to act in these ways? When students have practiced kindness and emotional regulation, they can learn how to bring these skills into social dynamics. With mindfulness students learn to communicate authentically and listen empathically. They can learn to check their assumptions and understand others with greater clarity and care.

Global Literacy

We tell our students to be aware of what is happening in the world and be good stewards of the earth, but how often do we teach them how to engage in these practices? Children can eventually extend their mindful kindness and attention to all things. They learn how the world affects them and how their actions affect the world. With an understanding of interconnectedness, students are empowered to be mindful ambassadors in the world.

MINDFUL REFLECTION WORKSHEET

This worksheet can be done at regular intervals for you and your students to learn how well the practices are working. Please remember that this is not a test or a way to grade students on their practice. We never want to give students the impression they will be judged on their capacity to be mindful. This should be offered as an opportunity for students to track the cultivation of their mindfulness skills. This is another form of mindfulness in which they can reflect on their minds.

You may offer this worksheet to students once a week or even at the end of every day. Then they can look through their reflections and see how they are developing in the practices. This is also a way for students to stop and reflect on their inner strengths. Each question is connected to a learning objective so we can see how different practices help students with specific faculties.

MINDFUL REFLECTION

What practices did you do today, when did you do them, and for how long?

_____

_____

_____

Stress Reduction: What was your stress level today?

STRESS MESS				NEUTRAL				CHILLING	
1	2	3	4	5	6	7	8	9	10

Focused Attention: How well were you able to focus today?

SPACED OUT				NEUTRAL				SAMURAI	
1	2	3	4	5	6	7	8	9	10

Empathy: How nice do you think you were to people today?

MEAN				NEUTRAL				KIND	
1	2	3	4	5	6	7	8	9	10

Resilience: How balanced were you today amidst adversity?

STRUGGLING				NEUTRAL				GRACEFUL	
1	2	3	4	5	6	7	8	9	10

Self-Compassion: How kind were you to yourself today?

HARSH				NEUTRAL				LOVING	
1	2	3	4	5	6	7	8	9	10

Contentment: How balanced was your mood today?

CHAOTIC				NEUTRAL				HAPPY	
1	2	3	4	5	6	7	8	9	10

Open-Mindedness: How aware were you today of the world around you?

MINDLESS				NEUTRAL				ATTUNED	
1	2	3	4	5	6	7	8	9	10

Emotional Self-Regulation: How was your impulse control today?

RECKLESS				NEUTRAL				VIGILANT	
1	2	3	4	5	6	7	8	9	10

Metacognition: How busy was your mind today?

FRENZIED				NEUTRAL				TRANQUIL	
1	2	3	4	5	6	7	8	9	10

Executive Functioning: How much drama did you get caught up in today?

CALAMITY				NEUTRAL				PEACEFUL	
1	2	3	4	5	6	7	8	9	10

Cognitive Flexibility: How easy were transitions for you today?

DISCOMBOBULATING				NEUTRAL				SMOOTH	
1	2	3	4	5	6	7	8	9	10

Physical
Literacy Lessons

PHYSICAL LITERACY

When taking attendance, we ask if students are present, but even when they are right there in front of us they are still often not very present. Really being present begins with the body. We learn to relax, feel the breath moving in and out, and explore the sensory map of our bodies. We get students ready to learn by helping them calm their nervous systems and anchor their attention in present-moment physical sensations so their minds are not wandering as much. Physical sensations are the building blocks for the rest of the mindfulness lessons. To focus we need to be able to anchor our attention on our present moment physical experience. To regulate emotions, we need to be able to be aware of how those emotions feel physically in the body. Therefore we consciously begin by offering students a foundation in physical awareness.

SHAKE IT OFF

To support students in feeling comfortable and relaxed in the classroom, we help their nervous systems find a state of rest. When there is a lot of dysregulation among students, we can use specific practices to help them relax and regulate. Here we explore some fun ways to bring awareness to our stress to find relaxation. We also create cognitive flexibility by shifting between chaos and stillness.

LEARNING OBJECTIVES

Stress reduction, impulse control, cognitive flexibility, contentment

Preparation and Considerations

Be particularly conscious with shaking practices that you are setting up a learning environment in which students will not bump into each other or hurt themselves. Find a big enough space for students to stand up and extend their arms in a circle without touching anyone or anything.

A rattle works well to begin and end the shaking time. You can use a shaker, a key chain, or extended sound such as a recorded song to signal when the movement should start and stop.

Lesson

We can begin by having students tighten up their bodies with each inhale and release with a big sigh on the exhale. We can have them tighten their fists, faces, and bodies as they inhale and then, as they breathe out, relax everything so that they are as loose as a noodle. Let them try tightening and relaxing for about 10 breaths. Then ask them to feel 10 breaths without tightening but while staying totally relaxed. Ask them how this felt.

Once they can tighten and relax, we can graduate to shaking. Have students stand up and start to shake their feet. Then have them shake their legs, up through the hips, the belly and chest, the arms, the head and neck, until their whole bodies are shaking. It can be nice to shake a rattle while they are moving.

At various moments we can call "freeze," or simply ask students to stop moving when the rattle stops. During these moments of pause, we can ask the group to notice what is happening in their bodies. Then we can call "shake" or begin rattling, and everybody will shake. Invite students to notice what it feels like inside their bodies when they are shaking, in stillness, and transitioning between states.

If the class is up for it, you can add blithering. This is when we let our tongues wag and make nonsense sounds. We can blither and shake our bodies at the same time. After a few alternating sessions of shaking and being still, ask the students what they noticed.

Dialogue Questions

What was the difference between feeling tense and feeling relaxed?

What was it like to shift between shaking and being still?

Inspiring Quote

66 *The mind should be allowed some relaxation, that it may return to its work all the better for the rest.* 99

—Seneca

Journaling Prompts

DRAWING: Draw one side of the paper in chaos and the other side of the paper calm and relaxed.

WRITING: Write about some moments in your life when you regularly feel stressed and some moments in your life when you feel calm.

Mindful Life Practice

Ask students to identify moments in their day when they feel tense or relaxed, chaotic or still. Ask if they can notice these moments when they occur and consciously switch from chaos to calmness. When they find themselves tense, they can mindfully relax; when they notice a lot of chaos; they can take a mindful pause.

Age and Stage

GRADES K–5: Younger students generally enjoy these exercises, especially when they are framed as games or when the practices go along with a story. Whenever we invite younger kids to shake their bodies and make silly noises, we need to ensure they don't knock into each other and that the class is regulated enough to come back to stillness after the shaking has begun.

GRADES 6–12: Adolescents and young adults need to understand the reason behind the practice. We can explain the neuroscience and health effects of stress and relaxation. Some students may feel too insecure to shake and blither. It's helpful to remind everyone to avoid looking at each other and that no one is required to do the practice.

LANGUAGE OF SENSATIONS

Learning the language of sensations in the body is foundational for mindfulness. In later lessons, knowledge of this language allows us to learn the language of the mind and the heart as well. The first step for teaching students the language of the body is to introduce them to an exploration of their own raw physical experience. We imagine our bodies as foreign countries we are visiting for the first time—we must learn both the language and the landscape. We must learn the language of our bodies before we can cultivate lasting impulse control, emotional regulation, and attention. By teaching this language, we help kids feel relaxed, safe, and at home in their own skin.

LEARNING OBJECTIVES

Focused attention, stress reduction, contentment, metacognition

Preparation and Considerations

For the following practice, it is preferable for students to be sitting on the floor or in chairs. An ideal space is one that feels safe and enjoyable with minimal distractions, and it is important to find the safest and most inspiring space. Children often lack the language to describe their sensations, so be patient in your exploration of sensation language. Rather than beginning the session by offering descriptions of what they may be feeling, let the students describe the experiences in their own way. Let them come up with metaphors, images, and other creative ways to describe their direct experiences. Provide some examples of what they may be feeling only if they are having trouble naming sensations by themselves; this will help them identify their experiences.

Lesson

Invite students to raise one hand and take a good look at it. Have them explore the lines, colors, and shapes as if they had never seen this hand before.

After a minute of examining the hand, ask them to keep holding it up in front of them while they close their eyes. We can ask, "Since your eyes are closed, how do you know your hand is there?"

After a minute of exploring the sensation in their hands, we can ask what they notice in their bodies. At this point you can begin making a list on the board of all the different sensations one can feel in a hand. Hot, cold, heavy, light, itchy, soft, damp, dry; students can fill in all types of ways one hand can feel.

To stimulate more sensations, we can have the children wiggle their fingers and observe the sensations that result. They can blow on their hands, lightly scratch with fingernails, rub a hand on a leg, touch the metal part of the desk, and other variations on these actions that will create different sensory experiences. We are creating a language for all of the ways our bodies can feel.

Dialogue Questions

Of the sensations we listed, which are your favorite?

Of the sensations we listed, which do you like the least?

Inspiring Quote

66 *Our bodies are our gardens to which our wills are gardeners.* 99

—William Shakespeare, *Othello*

Journaling Prompts

DRAWING: Draw a picture of your body. On every part of your body where you feel a sensation, make a mark with a color that fits the feeling.

WRITING: Make three lists of the sensations you feel in your body: one list for sensations you like, one list for those you don't like, and a third for sensations that are neutral.

Mindful Life Practice

Today, as you sit in class, notice the sensations in your body. Every few minutes, pause and notice the sensations in your hands. This can just take a few seconds.

Age and Stage

GRADES K–5: For elementary students, we can explore this lesson while sitting in a circle, or we can have students explore the sensations of their bodies at different times throughout the day, in different activities. Inviting children back to their direct physical experiences throughout the day offers them a solid foundation for learning the language of their bodies. Younger students will enjoy this practice if it is done playfully and as an inner body adventure. For example, we could have them imagine they are going on a submarine trip to investigate the sensations in their bodies.

GRADES 6–12: For middle and high school students, this lesson can last anywhere from half an hour to a full hour. The lesson simply asks students to sense particular parts of their bodies. Adolescents can have more in-depth discussions about their pleasant, unpleasant, and neutral experiences of different sensations. Teenagers will be able to reflect on the ways they are in relationship with their sensations. They may be more interested in imagining that they are scientists investigating the subtle cellular vibrations in the body.

PLAYING MINDFULNESS

We begin this practice with fun external movements. By the end of it, students are focused deeply on the feelings inside their own bodies, noticing subtle movements and stillness. Instead of simply instructing them to keep still, which may not be possible for them, we slowly bring them to a place where they notice the subtle ways their breath moves through their bodies.

LEARNING OBJECTIVES

Focused attention, stress reduction, impulse control, contentment, cognitive flexibility

Preparations and Considerations

It is important to make sure there is enough room for big movements—students must be able to swing their arms without hitting each other. Ideally, movements will be done standing up so the students can move their whole bodies. If the class is too rambunctious, these movements can be done sitting in chairs or on the floor. For students with disabilities, these practices can be done subtly by simply lifting the hands or turning the head.

Lesson

Begin by asking students if they have ever done the Spider-Man Breath. We invite students to breathe in with their hands close to their bodies, then, while breathing out, let their arms shoot out like Spider-Man shooting his webs. Lead them in a few in breaths with their arms pulling in, and then a few exhales shooting their webs out.

Then we invite students to do the Dolphin Breath. With each in breath, they curve their arms up in front of them like a dolphin jumping out of the water; with each exhale, they bring their arms down. Have students try a few of these breaths.

Now try the Crocodile Breath: on the in breath, they open their arms like the jaws of a crocodile; on the exhale, they clap their arms together. Have them try this a few times as well.

Then we can try a few Butterfly Breaths: let the wings (arms) open to the sides on the inhale and close together on the exhale.

Invite students to lift their shoulders up tight on the inhale and let them fall and totally relax on the exhale. Have them do this a few times.

Invite them to be totally still without moving a muscle. Welcome them to notice if they can feel anything moving, even while trying to keep everything immobile, as they breathe in and out.

Students love to come up with their own movements, and we can extend this game for a long time by having them make up elephant breaths, princess breaths, and anything else they invent that fits with the inhale and exhale. Begin with these fun, playful movements, then encourage smaller and smaller gestures. Students will become aware of the subtle movement of breath within their bodies when they are still.

Dialogue Questions

What movements do you notice in your body when you are trying to be totally still?

How does your body feel after doing the mindful movements?

Inspiring Quote

66 *We don't stop playing because we grow old, we grow old because we stop playing.* 99

—George Bernard Shaw

Journaling Prompts

DRAWING: Draw your favorite animal breathing.

WRITING: When you are totally still, what movements are happening in your body?

Mindful Life Practice

Ask students to notice the next time they feel stressed or worried, and take a moment to do the following exercise: breathe in and tighten up their shoulders, breathe out and relax and let it all go. Ask them to try this a few times and notice how it makes them feel.

We can also ask students to come up with some more mindful movements. They can think of other animals, imagine the ways they would breathe in and out, and practice those movements. Next time they come to class, they can share mindful movements with each other.

Age and Stage

GRADES K–5: Students at this stage enjoy the playfulness of animal movements and other games. Before we attempt attention lessons, we can use mindful movements to invite breath and stillness without prematurely encouraging students to be still and quiet.

GRADES 6–12: Students will engage with the mindful movements without needing the games. A good way of engaging older students is to explain the benefits of sports, dancing, or any other skill they want to develop. While the practice of playing mindfulness is aimed at younger students, there are many mindful movement practices that can be used for teenagers. Qigong, tai chi, yoga, and many martial arts movements are effective in helping older students connect with their bodies.

DEEP RELAXATION

Getting ready to learn necessitates that students feel relaxed and settled in their bodies. We can never know all of the stresses and traumas that our students are bringing to school. Mindful relaxation practice supports students in landing in the present moment, letting go of tensions and worries to show up fully for their learning. When the nervous system can relax, we can orient away from stressors and toward the lesson at hand.

LEARNING OBJECTIVES

Stress reduction, impulse control, contentment, well-being, self-compassion

---

Preparation and Considerations

To help students feel relaxed and safe, it is imperative to practice deep relaxation in a secure space with minimal distractions. Dim the lights if possible, play some soothing music, or figure out other ways for the room to feel calmer. If there is enough space, the students can lie down or sit relaxed in their chairs.

Lesson

We instruct students to begin by bringing their awareness to their heads, noticing any tension in their facial muscles, foreheads, or jaws. We have them accentuate the tension for a moment, tightening their muscles, and then fully relaxing with a big exhale. Have the students bring awareness to the sensations that come with every inhale and relax down into the ground with every exhale.

Instruct the students to bring their awareness to each point on their bodies from head to toe, taking 5 or 10 seconds at the neck, shoulders, and every other part of the body. At each area, students can note tension on the inhale and deeply relax on the exhale. We can scan from the head all the way down to the feet, progressively relaxing each area.

We can also focus on specific body areas with a lot of sensation, such as the hands, feet, face, and heart. We can ask students to notice the sensations in one hand, then the other, then both at the same time. Then we can have them bring their awareness to one foot, then the other, then both at the same time. Then they can notice their feet and hands all at once. We can even have them put their hands on certain areas to help them notice the sensations there.

After moving through the whole body, we can invite them to spend a few moments feeling their whole bodies fill up on the inhale and let go of any tension on the exhale. Give the students a moment to sit up and orient back to the room after their relaxation.

Dialogue Questions

Do you notice tension anywhere in your body?

When do you feel most relaxed?

Inspiring Quote –

❝ Tension is who you think you should be. Relaxation is who you are. ❞

—Chinese proverb

Journaling Prompts

DRAWING: Draw a picture of yourself resting in the safest and calmest scene you can imagine.

WRITING: Write down where you noticed tension in your body and what it felt like to relax.

Mindful Life Practice

We can invite students to practice this progressive relaxation when they are lying down to go to sleep. This practice can be particularly beneficial for kids who have trouble sleeping. We can also advise kids that whenever they feel stress building up in their bodies, they can take a moment to actively relax the places where they feel tension.

Age and Stage

GRADES K–5: Younger students generally enjoy being able to take a little rest. The younger the child, the less they may be able to follow the instructions to relax each part of the body. You may choose to have them relax their hands, their feet, their stomachs, and other more distinct spots so that you can be sure they are following along.

GRADES 6–12: For adolescents and young adults, it is helpful to lead off the lesson with a discussion about stress and a conversation about how the students experience it. When they understand why stress reduction is helpful, students will feel more invested in the practice. Some groups may not be open to lying down, and some classrooms may not allow for it. Sitting up is fine. When students get used to the practice, we can extend the lesson to 10 or 15 minutes of slowly moving through the body, relaxing every inch.

SLOW-MOTION MINDFULNESS

Mindful movement helps students bring relaxed awareness of their bodies into everyday experiences. It is important to practice in stillness and silence, but the goal of mindfulness is to teach us how to be present in the demands and activities of our daily lives. Slow-motion mindfulness is a beginning practice that leads us eventually to mindfulness as we play sports, walk to school, or fidget at our desks.

LEARNING OBJECTIVES

Stress reduction, focused attention, impulse control, metacognition

Preparation and Considerations

Depending on the group, we can choose different everyday objects that students use in their lessons, such as pencil and paper, a shoe, and play dough.

Students may start trying to compete by seeing who can move their bodies the slowest or get caught up in comparing their motions with others. Invite students to keep their attention on their own movements as much as possible.

Lesson

Invite students to put one hand on their desks or their knees. Then let them know that they will be moving the hand in slow motion all the way up to the sky and then back down. Ask them to see how slowly they can go. Explain that the point of the exercise is to experience what it feels like to move the hand so slowly. What do the bones, the skin, the tendons, and the whole mechanism of the arm feel like as the hand moves? Invite them to share aloud what the motion feels like after the exercise is done.

Then we move on to more complex motions. Ask the students to take out a piece of paper and a pencil. Ask them to become aware of their hands as they slowly lift and move their fingers toward the pencil, eventually touching, grasping, and lifting it. Invite them to be aware of every sensation in their fingers, the weight as the pencil lifts, and the particular posture the fingers are holding.

Welcome the students to write their names a couple of times, very slowly. Have them bring their awareness to the pressure of the pencil on the paper, the muscles and tendons moving in the hand, and the touch of the fingers on the pencil. From here we can explore lots of other common movements, such as slowly tying their shoes, opening a book, or twiddling their thumbs.

Let students know that they will be doing a slow-motion stand-up. Between sitting and standing there are many decisions to make: which leg to put the most weight on, whether to use a hand to push off from the desk, which ways the body will bend. We make most of these decisions without conscious thought. Invite the students to be as conscious as they can as they slowly stand up, noticing each sensation, each moving posture, and all the subtle balancing experiences.

If there is space and it seems like the students will be able to stay focused, have them practice some mindful walking. The students can form a circle and walk slowly, facing each other's backs. Or, if there is enough space, they can walk slowly around the room, in random patterns. Invite them to be aware of every lift and fall of their feet. Have them notice their balance and their breath as they walk. If possible, take the practice outdoors: mindful walking outside is especially nice.

Dialogue Questions

> **What did your body feel like moving so slow?**

> **Did you notice anything about the motion of walking that you usually don't notice?**

Inspiring Quote

66 *All that is important is this one moment in movement. Make the moment important, vital, and worth living. Do not let it slip away unnoticed and unused.* **99**

—Martha Graham

Journaling Prompts

DRAWING: Draw a picture of yourself performing an action you do every day, mindfully.

WRITING: Make a list of movements you perform throughout your day to which you could bring more mindfulness.

Mindful Life Practice

Ask students to choose one routine activity of their daily lives, such as brushing their teeth, opening the front door, or lying down to sleep. Have them try to remember this activity every day and bring awareness to it, noticing what their body feels like in the moment in which they engage in the activity. This will be an important way for them to begin bringing mindful awareness into their lives.

Age and Stage

GRADES K–5: It is important to make this practice fun for young students. We can have them play with play dough or checkers in slow motion. We can have them pretend to be sloths and reach their arms slowly toward a branch. Once students have had fun moving in slow motion, we can invite them to slow down their breath and notice the movement within their bodies. Even if we only do this for 10 seconds, it's a great way to teach kids how to slow down and look inside themselves.

GRADES 6–12: We can talk to older students about how easy it is to go on autopilot and how much better we can be at daily activities if we slow down and are more mindful in our movements. Older students will get on board when they realize this can help them with driving; playing sports, music, or videogames; or doing whatever else they are interested in. Find fun everyday activities that students can practice doing in slow motion, like pitching baseballs or typing.

Mental
Literacy
Lessons

MENTAL LITERACY

Cognitive research is mapping the benefits of mindfulness practice for executive functioning, working memory, attention control, and many other mental faculties. Through playing attention, students strengthen their focusing muscles by playing illuminating games. They get to open up the hood of their own minds and tinker around to maximize mental mechanics. In the following lessons, they learn about the mental phenomena of distraction, sustained attention, thought watching, and attuning the senses. Students can become empowered to build their attention to be better at school, sports, music, or whatever inspires them.

ANCHOR BREATHING

Mindful anchor breathing is a core lesson in mindfulness practice. We call this practice the anchor breath because the breath can be an anchor, a home base, to which we return at any time. Though the waves on the surface of our lives may be tumultuous, there is a stillness at the bottom of the ocean. The anchor breath can be our connection to that deep calm inside our bodies.

LEARNING OBJECTIVES

Executive functioning, emotional self-regulation, metacognition, focused attention, stress reduction, impulse control

Preparation and Considerations

It is crucial to conduct this exercise in a space with as few distractions as possible. It may be advisable to have students sit with some space between them to avoid distracting one another. For younger students, you can bring props to illustrate a boat and an anchor. It is important to let the children know there is no specific way that their breath is supposed to feel. The point of this exercise is to help them become aware of the sensory experience of breath, however it feels to them.

Lesson

Invite students to raise one hand and then bring it down to rest on their stomachs. Ask them to notice what is happening in their stomachs for a few breaths. This exercise arouses curiosity about the physical experience of breathing without telling them explicitly how to breathe.

Then invite students to see if they can sit really quietly and still, feeling the breath moving through their bodies. Ask them to note the four points of each breath, what we call the "diamond breath": the inhale, the full point, the exhale, and the empty point.

When teaching mindful breathing, it is helpful to explain that we build our focusing muscles on every breath. Recommend that students gently bring their minds back to the breath when they notice that they are thinking. Whatever arises—thoughts, emotions, sensations—welcome them without judgment and then bring the attention back to the breath.

After about a minute, or longer if it seems the students can continue to sit comfortably, ask them to open their eyes. When they are ready, have them share their experiences and talk about how they feel after the breathing practice. These questions are designed to elicit the students' experiences of following their breath and their reflections on what they noticed in their distracted minds.

Dialogue Questions

How do you imagine that mindful breathing might help you?

What did you notice about your mind?

Inspiring Quote

❝ Your mind is like this water, my friend: when it is agitated it becomes difficult to see. But if you allow it to settle, the answer becomes clear. ❞

—Oogway, *Kung Fu Panda*

Journaling Prompts

DRAWING: Draw a picture of an anchor that is settled in stillness beneath the rough waves of the ocean.

WRITING: Write about the ways your mind gets distracted and how you can bring it back to a place of calmness.

Mindful Life Practice

Ask students to practice the anchor breath for a few minutes every day, and use it whenever they feel upset, nervous, or otherwise uncomfortable. Before the next class, have them notice a moment when they feel annoyed or upset.

Point out that when something in their lives makes them upset, it creates a storm in their lives. Noticing this storm will give them the opportunity to remember their breath. Even when the waves are crazy, there can be calm stillness deep under the waves and in their bodies.

Age and Stage

GRADES K–5: Students need some more playfulness and guidance in this exercise. We can ask students if they know what an anchor is, and then spend some time making storm noises, and explain that when a storm comes, their boat needs an anchor so it won't get blown out to sea. Props can show how an anchor rests still beneath the waves even if the boat is getting blown around. Instead of trying the diamond breath, younger students may enjoy imagining their belly like a balloon getting bigger and smaller. Younger ones may benefit from lying on their backs and putting a teddy bear on their bellies as they breathe so they can notice it rising and falling with each breath.

GRADES 6–12: Students usually do not need much of a description of an anchor, but it's valuable to discuss with them the kinds of storms they experience in their lives, and what it would be like to have an anchor in troubling times. Older students can have in-depth conversations about what they notice in their distracted minds and how focusing could benefit them.

MINDFUL SEEING

With mindfulness we use an anchor to stabilize our awareness. The breath works well as this anchor, and there are many other anchor points we can use. One of the best anchor points students can use to cultivate their attention muscles is their eyes, in the practice of mindful seeing. Focusing the eyes on a single spot helps anchor awareness. When they get distracted and their eyes move, it is obvious to them that they have spaced out or become focused on something else.

LEARNING OBJECTIVES

Focused attention, executive functioning, impulse control, motivation, resilience

Preparations and Considerations

Classrooms often have posters, letters, and other pictures on the walls that can be used to focus the eyes. You can have all the students bring their attention to a single spot, such as a ball on the floor or a dot on the wall. If they are outside, students can look at a point on a tree's bark, a rock, or any other stationary object.

Though we are working to address the phenomenon of distraction, it is best to begin with as few external distractions as possible. Make sure that no one enters the classroom during this exercise, and students do not distract each other. Remember to tell them to avoid looking at any moving objects—especially each other.

There is a balance we want to help kids strike between being focused and being relaxed. If you see their eyes bugging out of their heads as they stare at the object of focus, remind them to relax their eyes.

Lesson

Draw a mark on the board or choose a spot that everyone can see. Have all the students look at the spot for 30 seconds without getting distracted.

Next have them stare at the spot for 30 seconds and tell them that this time you will try to distract them while they are looking. After a few seconds, start waving your hands next to the spot, picking up objects, and making funny movements. Ask what it was like for them to try to keep their eyes focused and what it was like to try to ignore the distraction.

Next have the class focus on the spot one more time and hold their attention there for 30 seconds. Have them relax their focus, releasing their stare from the one point so that they are not focusing on anything in particular, just seeing the whole room at once. We can shift a few times between focusing and relaxing the visual field. Ask the students what it was like to shift from focused to relaxed gaze.

Invite the students to see the world with new eyes: closing their eyes and, when they open them, imagining that this is the first time they have ever seen the room. Ask them to look around for a minute and see if they can spot anything they have never seen before.

Dialogue Questions

What did you notice about attention and distraction as you tried to focus?

Where else in your life could you practice seeing things with new eyes?

Inspiring Quote

" Everything has beauty, but not everyone sees it. "

—Confucius

Journaling Prompts

DRAWING: Look around the room and draw as many things as you can see.

WRITING: To what in your life would you like to give more attention?

Mindful Life Practice

Invite students to use their focusing eyes a few times a day to maintain focus on one object for a whole minute. We explain that the more they practice, the better they will get at focusing. You can become a mindful investigator by using mindful eyes to look around your home, the school, and the natural world to spot things you have never seen before.

Age and Stage

GRADES K–5: Students enjoy this exercise, especially if it's turned into a game. We can invite them to list the animals that have strong eyesight. Once they've done this, we can have them look around the room like these animals, looking as closely as they can at each object. Students as young as kindergarten can gain awareness of distractions through trying to focus on one spot and bringing their attention back when they realize it has wandered. The whole practice can last up to 15 to 20 minutes. It can be helpful to have young students choose an object, and then have a few students tell you what they have chosen so that you are sure they understand the directions.

GRADES 6–12: Students can use this practice to become aware of their distracted minds. You can ask questions like "Have you ever noticed how, when you are reading, your eyes sometimes go down the page without actually taking in the words?" This gives them a common example of distraction with which they might identify. You can help adolescents understand that they are building their attention muscles every time they return attention to their visual point of awareness.

MINDFUL LISTENING

We can anchor our experience to the present moment in many ways. We can feel our breath, smell a flower, listen to sounds, or pay attention to anything else that is happening right now. For this practice, we will become aware of the sounds around us. Active listening to sounds can be enough to engage our full attention. We just sit back and receive the waves of sound, almost as if we are sitting on a beach listening to the ocean waves hit the sand and recede, over and over.

LEARNING OBJECTIVES

Executive functioning, metacognition, focused attention, impulse control, open-mindedness, cognitive flexibility, developing memory

Preparation and Considerations

For this lesson we need a musical instrument that makes a long, sustained, gentle sound. You could also use a prerecorded song. As we continue to teach this practice, it can be fun to find different instruments for the students to listen to, such as rattles, rain sticks, and different kinds of bells. Eventually it can be nice to bring students outside to listen to the many noises of their environment, but at first, it is helpful to have them in a quiet space where they can really focus on one sound.

Lesson

We begin the lesson by letting students know that today we will be using our ears to focus. They are already using their mindful listening skills as they listen to our instructions. We will be strengthening their listening with this practice.

Introduce the students to the instrument that will be used. Let them know that we sit tall and relaxed in our mindful bodies to listen to the sound. We listen to the full duration of the sound and then lift a hand up in the air when we can't hear it anymore.

The next time we practice, try closing our eyes and being very still and quiet to see if we can hear the sound even longer.

Next we listen to the sound again, but this time we won't lift our hands when it ends. Instead, we keep listening to the other sounds we hear. We can direct students to hear the sounds that are far away, such as airplanes and distant cars. Then they can focus on more immediate sounds, such as the buzz of the heater or the creak of a chair.

Remind students that if a thought comes into their heads, they should let it rise up like the sound of a car going by and then fade away, continuing to come back to listening.

We can also make the practice into a game. Students start by listening to the room with their eyes closed. Then, we can make some noises in the midst of silence—tapping our fingers on the desk, rubbing our hands together, shaking our keys—and have the students guess what the sounds are.

Dialogue Questions

How do you feel after practicing the exercise?

What did you notice about your minds as you tried to pay attention?

Inspiring Quote

66 *We have two ears and one mouth so that we can listen twice as much as we speak.* 99

—Epictetus

Journaling Prompts

DRAWING: Draw a picture as if you could see the sounds you are hearing right now.

WRITING: Write what you notice about your attention when you try to stay focused on sound.

Mindful Life Practice

Throughout the week invite students to keep their mindful ears open and see if they notice any noises they usually miss. If they've been forgetting to really listen in their lives, they may be amazed by the sounds all around them. Ask students to come into class with three sounds they heard in their everyday life that they had not noticed before.

Age and Stage

GRADES K–5: Students will enjoy this practice when it is more playful. We can ask kids to listen and see how many different sounds they can hear. We can play different bells, and have the students guess, with their eyes closed, which bells we are playing and in what order. Young minds tend to wander easily if there is nothing on which their attention can focus, so ringing a bell that has a long duration of sound is helpful for younger students. The practice of following the sound and raising their hands when they cannot hear it anymore really helps them stay focused in the present.

GRADES 6–12: Students can focus on sound for five minutes or longer. This is another way for adolescents to imagine building their attention muscles. It is important to help them remember that the moment they realize their minds are wandering—that they are no longer registering sounds and are listening to the thoughts in their heads—they are missing the music of the world. This is a great practice with which to open and end classes. Older students can begin practice noticing how their bodies and emotions respond to each sound.

POPCORN THOUGHTS

The following practice works well for any age group. It increases students' ability to witness their own thoughts, helping create some space between thoughts and actions—the space, for instance, between the thought "I don't like that guy" and the action of coldly excluding him from the group or worse yet hitting him. In this brief reflective moment, students gain objectivity regarding their thoughts and consequently make better decisions. When we help kids expand this space, we give them the opportunity to self-regulate.

> ## LEARNING OBJECTIVES
> **Executive functioning, metacognition, focused attention, impulse control, open-mindedness, resilience, cognitive flexibility**

Preparation and Considerations

Once students have cultivated the ability to stabilize their awareness using the anchor breath, they will be ready to give this practice a try. They must be familiar with the concept of bringing one's attention back to an anchor before they are able to witness their thoughts. We need to make sure the room is quiet and contains no disruptions.

Remember not to judge specific thoughts as good or bad. Whether happy thoughts, disturbing thoughts, or creative thoughts arise, they all can simply be noticed as "popping" thoughts.

Lesson

Invite students to sit tall and relaxed. Let them know we will be learning about our brains today. Tell them that our minds are much like a popcorn maker—but instead of making popcorn, they make thoughts. Thoughts are just popping left and right, nonstop.

Begin by asking the students to sit mindfully for 20 seconds with eyes closed and trying not to have any thoughts.

Then ask the students to put one hand on their bellies to bring their attention back to their breath and let them know we will be using the anchor breath. Whenever a thought comes into their heads, students can pop their hands up. Then they can bring their hands back to their bellies and rest their attention back on their breath.

Dialogue Questions

When each thought comes to you, how does it affect your body, your breath, and your emotions?

Where do you think your thoughts come from?

Inspiring Quote ─ ─ ─ ─ ─ ─ ─ ─ ─ ─ ─ ─ ─ ─ ─

Don't believe everything you think.

—Unknown

Journaling Prompts

DRAWING: Draw a bunch of popcorn popping. In each popcorn kernel, draw a little picture of what you thought about during the mindfulness practice.

WRITING: Write about where you think thoughts come from.

Mindful Life Practice

Suggest to students that they try to notice their thoughts wherever they are, that they work on witnessing them as passing, popping thoughts and continue to come back to their breath. Whether they are on the playground or at home, they can watch their thoughts and decide what they want to do with them. When they witness their thoughts, they may find a greater sense of stillness and relaxation. Instead of being caught in the storm of thinking, they notice angry, excited, or sad thoughts and simply come back to the breath.

Age and Stage

GRADES K–5: Students can gain the capacity for self-reflection through fun thought games. We can bring a snow globe to the classroom, shake it up so that the scene inside of the globe is muddled, and then put it on the table where it can gently settle. We can let students know that as they practice their mindful breathing and watch the globe, the snowflakes are settling just like the thoughts are settling in their heads. This practice allows them to see, calmly, what's really inside their minds. Simple exercises like these offer young children the profound ability to become aware of their own thought processes.

GRADES 6–12: Students can become aware of their thinking processes and then go a step or two further. Depending on their age and capacity, they can learn to watch their thoughts and become aware of which emotions arise when thoughts come. They may get excited by certain thoughts and angered by others. They may notice that whenever they think of eating food they get excited and when they think of tests, they feel anxious. Once they can track this process, they will gain a high level of self-reflection and self-regulation.

THE DISTRACTION GAME

With this practice, students get a clear understanding of how their minds wander even as they try to keep a sharp focus. Once they can reflect on their own attention, emotions, and bodies, as they have learned to do in previous lessons, we can begin to play with the ways the mind gets carried away. This game is especially helpful when students are distracted by, for example, their friends or sounds outside the room; you can show them how to work with these types of distractions. It is one thing to stay mindful when everything is quiet; this practice helps us be mindful amidst the chaos of everyday life.

LEARNING OBJECTIVES

Executive functioning, metacognition, focused attention, resilience, motivation, impulse control

---

Preparation and Considerations

During the class we will be making noises and will need to have space to walk around the room. In many classrooms there are boxes of pencils, books, and other objects to make noises with. We can also use some shakers, bells, or other noisemaking tools.

Be sure that students have already developed comfort and skill in exercises involving the body, the anchor breath, and awareness of thoughts.

When playing the distraction game, it is important to remember that certain students have nervous systems that are more sensitive than others. Be sure to avoid making loud or abrupt noises and keep an especially watchful eye on the class.

Lesson

Begin by asking students what the word *distraction* means. Then let the students know that we will be playing the distraction game today. Ask who thinks that they will be able to sit mindfully and practice their anchor breath even while we are trying to distract them. We can choose one student and invite her to sit still with her eyes closed, focusing on her breath. Let the other students know they can focus on their own breath as well and support the volunteer by being very mindful and quiet.

Then we can make all sorts of distracting noises such as shaking a pencil jar, tapping our fingers on a desk, or stepping loudly across the floor. After a minute we can give an appreciation to the volunteer for her efforts, even if she became distracted.

Then ask who else would like to play the distraction game and go through the same process with the entire class. Invite everyone to focus on their breath while we go around the room making noises. Try this for a couple of minutes, reminding students to stay focused on their breath without getting distracted by the sounds.

Next ask for a volunteer to be the distracter's assistant. Usually some of the kids who are the biggest classroom distracters raise their hands, and we can intentionally choose one of them. Create a set-up in which the student who is usually trying to distract other kids is actively doing this and students who are trying not to get distracted are actively working their attention muscles.

Make sure the distracter knows not to touch anyone or make noises that are too loud. Walk around the room with the distracter, trying to distract students while they practice their mindful breathing. It's wonderful to have enough time to play with distraction over the course of several classes, so that each student feels what it is like to distract and be distracted. This empowers them, allowing them to understand what distraction and impulsivity feel like on the inside.

Dialogue Questions

What does distraction feel like in your bodies?

What are some ways in which you distract others?

Inspiring Quote

❝ *You will never reach your destination if you stop and throw stones at every dog that barks.* ❞

—Winston S. Churchill

Journaling Prompts

DRAWING: In the middle of the page, draw a picture of yourself mindfully sitting. Then draw lots of distractions all around you.

WRITING: Write about the ways that you get distracted and what would help you stay focused.

Mindful Life Practice

Tell the students they can use the distraction game in their lives as an opportunity to come back to their attention. We might suggest they schedule moments throughout the day, such as when a bell rings at school or a phone rings at home, to take three mindful breaths. Every time they hear a loud noise or someone walks into the room, they have an opportunity to notice the distraction and return to their anchor breath. This doesn't mean that they should ignore the sound, but they shouldn't get lost in thoughts about it. They can practice this wherever they are, especially when reading, playing the piano, or doing anything else that takes focus. Encourage them to see how distractions affect them and use distractions as opportunities to strengthen their "attention muscles."

Age and Stage

GRADES K–5: Students usually love playing this game, which has many variations and can be played again and again. When a child or the whole class seems particularly distracted, we can ask if they want to play the distraction game.

GRADES 6–12: Students can take the basic premise of this game and go much further. We can say funny things as the students are focusing and ask them to keep their attention on their breath rather than getting lost in the words. We can get different students to say funny things and have the students practice maintaining their anchor breath. This becomes a great way to practice together.

Emotional
Literacy
Lessons

EMOTIONAL LITERACY

Emotional regulation has been shown to be a profound predictor for academic achievement as well as success in many realms of life. Shouldn't we be taking the emotional health of our students as a major focus of our education? With these lessons we help students to navigate the realm of emotions, regulating the difficult ones and enhancing the healthy ones. Students learn to notice the ways difficult emotions feel in their bodies and create impulse control and self-regulation skills. They can generate gratitude, happiness, and empathy by learning how to use emotions to feel good and be good. We can call the following lessons heartfulness lessons, in which we are regulating and strengthening the heart.

HEARTFUL PHRASES

Speaking heartful phrases generates kindness for ourselves and others. We are seeking to cultivate generosity and good will within ourselves. When we say, "I wish for your happiness," we find genuine care for others and ourselves in our hearts. Even if we don't feel happy at a particular moment, we can usually get in touch with at least a desire for happiness. This desire is what fuels heartful phrases. We can genuinely say, "I wish to be happy," especially when we are not feeling good. It takes courage to care for ourselves in this way, and this courage can transform classroom environments.

LEARNING OBJECTIVES

Contentment, empathy, self-compassion, prosocial behavior, focused attention, open-mindedness, cognitive flexibility

Preparation and Considerations

It is necessary to have practiced language of sensations and popcorn thoughts prior to this lesson. Having an anchored awareness and an understanding of sensations in the body sets the foundation for students to gain a greater understanding of how emotions work. It's helpful to hold these classes in a safe and contained space. Remind students that everything shared in the lesson is confidential.

Lesson

Let students know that we are going to explore a new type of lesson called heartfulness. We can remind them that mindfulness is all about using our minds to pay closer attention to our senses, our thoughts, our breath, and the world around us. We can ask students what they think heartfulness might be about. Then we can let them know that we will enter the landscape of the heart, paying attention to our emotional intelligence.

Have students begin by simply putting their hands on their hearts and seeing what they feel in there. Invite them to take some nice long breaths and notice what they feel in their chests.

Invite students to send themselves some positive thoughts. Have them continue holding their hands to their hearts or give themselves a big hug and send themselves some good wishes. Offer up some examples for them to repeat, such as "I wish to be happy," "I wish to feel healthy," and "I wish to feel confident." Invite students to come up with their own positive wishes for themselves to say inward or share with the group.

From here we begin the practice of sending our good wishes out to others. Ask students to look around at their fellow classmates and send them good wishes. We begin with some phrases they can share while looking around at each other such as, "I wish you have a happy day," "I wish you have lots of friends," and "I wish for you to be awesome!" Have students look around and wish good things for each other.

Then we open our arms wide or take a moment to think of the diverse people in our vast world and send them good wishes. Students can think of kids, adults, and even animals and say things like, "I wish for the world to find peace where there is violence," "I wish there is food for those who are hungry," "I wish there is joy in the hearts of those who are troubled," and "I wish for the oceans, and the forests, and all the animals to be healthy." We can ask students to continue making their positive wishes to send out to the world.

Dialogue Questions

How does this practice make you feel in your body?

Why is it important to think kind thoughts about others?

Inspiring Quote

— — — — — — — — — — — — — — —

" *The giving of love is an education in itself.* "

—Eleanor Roosevelt

— — — — — — — — — — — — — — —

Journaling Prompts

DRAWING: Draw a picture of happiness spreading around the world.

WRITING: Write a list of wishes you have for yourself, your community, and the world.

Mindful Life Practice

Let students know to begin by cultivating heartfulness for themselves. Every night before they go to bed and every morning when they wake up, they can say some good wishes and be kind to themselves. Let them know it is possible to totally change the attitude they carry throughout the day by using these phrases. Explain how it's like brushing our teeth every morning and night, but we're spending time strengthening and taking care of our hearts. Invite them to give it a try and see how it affects them.

Age and Stage

GRADES K–5: Students enjoy coming up with wishes to send to themselves and others, so it is a game they are happy to repeat regularly. Students can give themselves a big hug when they are sending themselves good wishes. Then have them put their hands out in front of them as they look around the room and send good wishes to each other. Finally, have them open their arms wide so they can send wishes around the whole world. With younger students, it often works well to have them repeat the good wishes out loud in a call and response.

GRADES 6–12: Students often don't think it's cool to be nice to themselves or others. When speaking to teenagers, it can be helpful to talk about how everyone just wants to be happy and have people be nice to them, but because of our lack of emotional intelligence, we are sometimes mean to ourselves and others. Once older students learn to send kind and caring thoughts to themselves and the people they care about, they can send caring thoughts to people who annoy them, or to those with whom they have had conflicts. This becomes a practice of forgiveness and heart-opening.

ROOTS OF EMOTIONS

In this lesson we support students in understanding the relationships between their thoughts, emotions, and sensations. We begin by teaching students how to relax and regulate their bodies when they are stressed with a breathing practice we call the vacuum breath. Once students know how to de-stress, we teach them to track what happens inside them when they get upset so that they know when to use the vacuum breath to self-regulate. We instruct them on how to understand how their emotions function, demonstrating how to find the emotional root behind those moments when their minds are spinning with thoughts. Students learn to stop worrying or stewing in anger and feel the emotions in their bodies. When they can bring a calming breath to the uncomfortable sensations, they can release themselves from distressing thoughts and mind-sets.

LEARNING OBJECTIVES

Empathy, executive functioning, emotional self-regulation, metacognition, focused attention, stress reduction, resilience, self-compassion, open-mindedness, contentment, cognitive flexibility

Preparation and Considerations

This practice may bring up emotions for students. Make sure to conduct the lesson in a contained space and remind the class of confidentiality. When emotions arise, you have a great opportunity to support the students, letting them know that everything is welcome in the class and there are no judgments on emotions. It is necessary to have practiced the language of sensations as well as popcorn thoughts. We want students to already have a good grasp of how they feel their emotions in their bodies and be able to witness their thoughts.

Lesson

Let students know that this lesson will help them work with their emotions by tracking their thoughts and feelings, realizing when they are triggered, and learning to relax and let go.

Invite students to begin by sitting in a mindful posture. We invite them to sit with their eyes closed and focus on the sensations in their bodies. Have the students bring their awareness to different parts of their bodies and notice any tension or stress. Have them breathe in and notice the weather pattern in their head, in their shoulders, in their hands, their stomachs, and other zones where we often feel tension.

Then introduce the vacuum breath. Invite students to imagine that there is a vacuum cleaner in their stomachs that can suck up any tension or stress. As they take a long inhale, they can imagine that any stress from their heads, shoulders, chests, is getting sucked down into the bottom of their bellies. Then they can hold the breath for three seconds in the belly, and when they release imagine they are releasing any gunk down into the ground.

After students have practiced the vacuum breath, we can invite them to imagine a recent moment when they felt a little annoyed or frustrated. As they are picturing this scene, they should notice how it affects their bodies. Are their shoulders tight? Does their breath quicken? Is their face hot?

When they notice how the frustrating experience affects their bodies, they can begin practicing the vacuum breath, pulling all the tension from their bodies into their stomachs and then releasing it down into the Earth. Invite students to notice anywhere there is tension, breathe it into the belly, hold the breath there for three seconds, and then let it go.

Dialogue Questions

In what ways might you feel different now than when you started this practice?

Why do you think that we sometimes do and say things we wish we hadn't?

Inspiring Quote

« A crust eaten in peace is better than a banquet partaken in anxiety. »

—Aesop

Journaling Prompts

DRAWING: Draw a picture of yourself releasing all the stress from your body.

WRITING: Write about when you might be able to use this practice in your everyday life.

Mindful Life Practice

Now that the students have experienced the vacuum breath, they can do it anywhere. Remind them that when they get angry at their siblings, or their parents won't let them do something they really want to do, or if they are scared as they are facing a new challenge, they can use the vacuum breath. Have them do it over the next few days and share about it during the next mindfulness lesson.

Age and Stage

GRADES K–5: Students can do a shortened variation of this practice. The visual of a vacuum cleaner in the belly pulling in all the uncomfortable feelings is helpful for students at this age. The practice can be very beneficial for students and the whole class when there is a lot of stress in the room: before a test, for instance, or after a conflict between students. When doing the body scan with younger children, allow only a minute or so to go through the whole body, exploring unpleasant feelings.

GRADES 6–12: Students can explore in depth the intricacies of how emotions can be felt as physical sensations. It can be extremely liberating for students to track their emotional thoughts through their bodies, where they can relax them and let them go. With older students, you can take time during the body scan to feel into each body area, noticing stress, pain, and unpleasant emotions, and tend to them with the breath.

DIFFICULT EMOTIONS

Once we have opened the door to our emotions, we can begin to work with those that are difficult in addition to those that are easy or pleasant. If we don't know how to navigate emotions such as anger, sadness, and fear, they can be very destructive. We assume these emotions will visit our hearts at some point, and we use heartfulness to prepare for them: instead of getting disturbed when they arrive, we can learn and grow from the experience.

LEARNING OBJECTIVES

Emotional self-regulation, focused attention, stress reduction, resilience, open-mindedness, contentment, cognitive flexibility

Preparations and Considerations

This practice should come after learning the language of sensations, anchor breath, and roots of emotion. Students should already have an anchor to which they feel safe coming back. Again, it is imperative that we create an emotionally and physically safe space, that everyone agrees to confidentiality, and that resources are available in case lots of emotions arise for any students. We want to be careful not to bring up emotions that are too intense. Whenever strong feelings bubble up, tell students that their anchor breath is right there to support them.

Lesson

Let students know that today we are taking a mindfulness journey into our emotions. We start at our base camp of mindful breathing and explore different emotional states, always with the option of coming back to base camp when we need to. Invite students to practice their mindful vacuum breath for a minute or so.

Share how everyone experiences fear, anger, sadness, and other difficult emotions now and then. We assume these hard feelings will arrive sometimes. What's important is what we do when they knock on the door.

As the students are mindfully breathing, ask them to imagine they are standing up, walking out the door, and heading off to play their favorite game or do a favorite activity. They can imagine this sequence as if they were watching a movie in their minds. After this visualization, ask the students what it feels like in their bodies when they picture this scene.

Next invite students to imagine that someone comes to them and angrily tells them they have to stop what they are doing. Have the students picture this scene and notice how it affects their bodies. After this visualization, have them practice a few vacuum cleaner breaths.

Now invite students to imagine they are coming back to school and there is a pop quiz they haven't studied for. As they picture themselves sitting down to take the quiz, have them notice how their body feels. Then invite them to take a few vacuum breaths.

Then have the students imagine that they get the quiz back and have received a perfect score! Have them imagine this and notice how they feel. Then have them imagine that their friend got a perfect score as well, and tells them so. Have the students see if they can feel empathic excitement for their friend. Have them see what it feels like in their bodies to feel good about someone else's success.

Dialogue Questions

How did you feel in your body when you imagined going out to play?

How did you feel in your body when you imagined being given the pop quiz?

Inspiring Quote

66 One ought to hold on to one's heart;
for if one lets it go, one soon loses control of the head too. 99

—Friedrich Nietzsche

Journaling Prompts

DRAWING: Imagine being given a pop quiz or some stressful situation. Then draw an outline of your body, and fill it in with shapes and colors to show the emotions you feel inside your body.

WRITING: Write down a bunch of adjectives that describe what your body feels like when you are stressed. For each one, write something specific that can help relax or release that stress.

Mindful Life Practice

Now that students know how to witness emotions in their bodies, they have an amazing tool they can carry with them wherever they go. Remind them that when they feel scared, sad, or anything else that's difficult or unpleasant, they can become aware of the feeling in their bodies and then do some mindful breathing. They can also begin to become aware of how they feel in different places and with different people. Explain that once they do this type of investigation, they can choose experiences that make them happy.

Age and Stage

GRADES K–5: Students usually enjoy going on an imaginary journey. We can set up all types of scenarios for them. Some teachers lead collaborative imaginary journeys through the jungle or space. They tell the students they are going on a safari and all the students get to imagine another world together, choosing the adventure as they go. Bringing students back to noticing what they are feeling in their bodies is what makes this a mindfulness practice. This practice helps young children become aware of the emotions that arise in different situations and how to regulate their systems.

GRADES 6–12: Students can learn a great deal from this practice. Instead of going on safari, the metaphors can be more focused on experiences that frustrate them. When students witness the sensations that arise in difficult moments, they begin to gain control of their responses. This leads to some fascinating conversations for older students. We can even make a list of situations that students find scary, frustrating, exciting, and happy, and use these situations for visualization exercises.

GENERATING GRATITUDE

What are you grateful for? This question invites a mind-set that appreciates what the world has already offered us, rather than focusing on the things we lack. Each breath has been gifted by the trees and plants. Our food is a gift from the plants and animals. Looking at the miraculous phenomenon of life can awaken gratitude, love, and compassion within us.

LEARNING OBJECTIVES

Empathy, executive functioning, emotional self-regulation, metacognition, focused attention, resilience, self-compassion, contentment, cognitive flexibility

Preparation and Considerations

Prepare gratitude journals for the class or have students make their own.

Remember to be sensitive to the diversity of our students. We would not instruct them to be grateful for "parents," as some students may not have them. Find basic examples for objects of gratitude, such as breath, water to drink, and sunshine.

Gratitude practice in a group is especially meaningful. A group begins each day by saying what they are most grateful for in their lives and ends each day saying what they were most grateful for that day in class.

Lesson

Let students know that today we will be learning about the power of gratitude. When we are grateful, we shift our attention from those things that are not good enough in our lives and focus on the millions of little things that are needed for us to be alive in this moment.

Explain how often we forget all the things in our lives that we can be grateful for. Compare this forgetfulness to that of a rock at the top of a pyramid that forgets about all the rocks it is sitting on. Remind students that we are alive because so many ancestors before us survived and fell in love and did so many things that allowed us to be here today. Talk to students about how the sun has to keep rising every day to give life to the plants that we need to breath and to eat. Remind them about the people who clean the bathrooms we use, deliver the food to the store where we buy it, and build the buildings in which we learn.

Welcome students to let their eyes close and put on their mindful bodies. They can begin be returning to their mindful breathing. Once they feel calm, have them picture one of their heroes or a person in their lives who makes them feel really happy. They can imagine that this person is sitting right next to them. Invite them to notice what it feels like to imagine the person there.

Have students picture a few more heroes and special people in their lives and imagine them all sitting around them, looking at them with big smiles and encouragement. Let them share what it is like to be surrounded by caring heroes.

Now students can picture their favorite food and imagine it is right in front of them. Have them imagine the colors and the smells and notice what their bodies feel like as they do so.

Now they can think of everything at once: their favorite things, their favorite people, the things for which they are most grateful. They can picture all these things around them. Invite them to notice what it feels like to picture this.

Now they can take a deep breath, let go of all the things for which they are grateful, and simply notice what their bodies feel like after this gratefulness practice.

Dialogue Questions

What are you grateful for?

What are some things, like the sun and the rain, that you need to live?

Inspiring Quote ‐

❝We can complain because rose bushes have thorns, or rejoice because thorn bushes have roses.❞

—Abraham Lincoln

‐ ‐

Journaling Prompts

DRAWING: Draw a picture of yourself surrounded by all the people for whom you are most grateful.

WRITING: Write a list of the aspects of yourself for which you are most grateful.

Mindful Life Practice

Once students have been introduced to a gratitude practice, they can begin their own gratitude journal. They can keep this journal indefinitely or for a limited time. Encourage them to write an entry every day about the things and people they are grateful for. During a future class session, make time to discuss the things they have noticed about themselves and the world since they've started keeping the journal.

Age and Stage

GRADES K–5: Students can easily enter into both visualization and sharing about what they are grateful for. The practice can be done as a check-in every morning, in a circle. It can also be done in the afternoon as a way to share what students were most grateful for during the day. Weaving gratitude into the classroom creates an environment of appreciation and kindness.

GRADES 6–12: Students can engage in fascinating discussions about cultivating positive mind states as a result of this practice. A good group discussion to return to regularly is how we can choose to focus on what we are grateful for or what we are upset about. Describing the neuroscience around positive mind states can be very productive with older students.

POSITIVE QUALITIES

We can tell students to pay better attention, be kind, and control their impulses, but these concepts can be elusive. With mindfulness, we support students to build the positive qualities they need to thrive. Here we offer students direct experiences of what it feels like in their bodies to pay close attention or be a person who is genuinely kind. Students can choose which qualities they want to develop and then explore an accessible method for growth.

> ## LEARNING OBJECTIVES
>
> **Emotional self-regulation, executive functioning, metacognition, empathy, focused attention, stress reduction, resilience, open-mindedness, contentment, cognitive flexibility**

Preparation and Considerations

Prior to leading the practice, decide on a few positive qualities to highlight during the session. For younger students, we may bring in pictures of animals that exemplify focus, kindness, or motivation. For older students, we can bring in pictures or video clips of people who exemplify positive qualities. We may bring in a picture of a tightrope walker to demonstrate focus or a picture of Mother Teresa feeding children for kindness. Invite students to think about the qualities they would like to cultivate in themselves, rather than telling them which ones we think they need to develop.

Lesson

Tell students about the many wonderful qualities we have inside of us, such as kindness, motivation, and peacefulness. Share some stories of people or animals that exemplify these qualities.

We can begin with the quality of motivation. Ask students who, among the people they know, exemplifies the quality of motivation. We may give some examples of mountain climbers or dedicated ballet dancers.

Have the students put on their mindful bodies and imagine someone who personifies motivation in their minds. Invite them to close their eyes and picture this person doing something with true determination and motivation. Then have the students picture themselves in this person's shoes. Have them imagine they are the personification of motivation. Then have the students check into their bodies and see what it feels like to be so motivated.

Next invite the students to think of someone who personifies kindness. Invite them to imagine this person and picture them doing kind deeds and going through their day with kindness. They can put themselves into this person's shoes and imagine they are this kind and generous. Have them check into their bodies and see what it is like to be so kind.

Then invite the students to imagine someone who is very peaceful. Whether life is chaotic or calm, this person stays balanced. Have them picture this person going through their day and notice how he or she acts. They can imagine themselves in the shoes of this peaceful person and see what it feels like to be so balanced.

We can move through lots of positive qualities with students and have them think of the qualities they want to cultivate most. Then they can picture the person who exemplifies the quality they want to strengthen in themselves, and use this person to charge the batteries of that specific quality. If, for example, students want to cultivate more focus, they can call to mind their focus mentor. If they want to build kindness, they can picture their kindness mentor.

Dialogue Questions

How did each of these different qualities feel different in your bodies?

Which qualities do you want to cultivate the most?

Inspiring Quote

**❝ *Nurture your mind with great thoughts.*
To believe in the heroic makes heroes. ❞**

—Benjamin Disraeli

Journaling Prompts

DRAWING: Draw a picture of yourself as a superhero whose power is a positive quality.

WRITING: Write down a list of positive qualities. Think about which ones you're already embodying, and those with which you could use some practice.

Mindful Life Practice

We can support students in choosing which positive qualities they want to cultivate. If a student wants to be more motivated, we can invite them to practice once a day by bringing a motivational mentor into their minds, imagining themselves as this mentor and then feeling the motivation in their bodies. Explain that they can use this practice whenever they want to build attention, compassion, peacefulness, or any other positive quality.

Age and Stage

GRADES K–5: Students will enjoy this practice if they are introduced to it in engaging ways. We can have them talk about which animals or superheroes exemplify different qualities. Then the students imagine themselves as these animals or superheroes. Have the students draw pictures of characters who embody positive qualities or act them out. It's important to remember to stop the students after they have spent some time exploring these qualities and ask them how they feel inside. This will help them feel what it is like to pay attention, be kind, or express whatever quality they are acting out.

GRADES 6–12: Students can practice deeper self-reflection and begin to assess which qualities they want to cultivate. It is helpful to walk students through many different qualities and lead discussions about each one. Then they can assess how they need to grow and can commit to practicing and building their positive qualities. For older students, it can be helpful to mention celebrities or public leaders who may personify these qualities as additional examples.

Social Literacy Lessons

SOCIAL LITERACY

Bullying, social ostracizing, racism, and other forms of social mindlessness are deeply troubling to individuals and our larger society. With the following practices, we aim at supporting students' capacities for empathy, open-mindedness, and communication skills and creating a mindful community together. We use the capacities we have already built in looking at our thoughts and emotions to become aware of our unconscious assumptions, look at one another with understanding, and cultivate kindness. With these practices, we inspire students to bring the beautiful inner mindful qualities they have developed into the world to enact positive change.

JUST LIKE ME

As students learn to build their heartfulness, they start to open their hearts to others. We teach students to gain an empathic understanding of another person's world. Instead of simply telling them to be nice to each other, we offer them an experiential window into other students' hearts. This allows them to make future life choices from a place of compassion and understanding.

LEARNING OBJECTIVES

Empathy, executive functioning, emotional self-regulation, focused attention, self-compassion, open-mindedness, contentment, cognitive flexibility

Preparation and Considerations

When practicing heartfulness, we want to create a secure space with minimal interruptions. We want students to know that anything that is shared in the space will stay within the group. As much as possible, we want to create an emotionally safe space where students can feel comfortable enough to be vulnerable.

Lesson

Invite students to come back to their base of breath, feeling it move in their bodies.

Have students begin by sending themselves some of the good wishes they learned in a previous lesson. We can give some examples, such as "May I be happy, "May I be safe," and "May I be strong and healthy." They can send other good thoughts to themselves as they like.

Next have students think of one of their favorite people: a friend, a family member, maybe even a pet. Then they can send these same wishes to this person or animal: "Just like me, this person wants to be happy," "Just like me, this person wants to be safe," "Just like me, this person wants to be strong and healthy." They continue picturing the person and saying more "Just like me" phrases, by themselves.

Finally we ask them to picture someone who annoys them a little bit. We can tell them to picture this person, whether it's someone in class, a sibling, or even a teacher, and as they picture this person they can say the same phrases and see if they really believe it: "Just like me, this person wants to be happy," "Just like me, this person wants to be safe," "Just like me, this person wants to be strong and healthy." They continue picturing the person and saying more "Just like me" phrases.

Dialogue Questions

What did it feel like to send good wishes to people with whom you are annoyed?

Why do you think it's important to practice empathy?

Inspiring Quote

Three things in human life are important.
The first is to be kind. The second is to be kind.
The third is to be kind.

—Henry James

Journaling Prompts

DRAWING: Draw a picture of yourself doing something kind for others.

WRITING: Write about someone you know and make a list of all the things that you could say or offer to them that would make them happy.

Mindful Life Practice

Ask students to choose an act of kindness they can perform in their lives: for example, opening the door for others, being friendly to a student who often sits by themselves, or committing not to put anyone down for a whole day. See what creative ideas they come up with.

Age and Stage

GRADES K–5: Younger students will need to be walked through this project without too much time spent in silence. They can repeat after us when we say our phrases of kindness to ourselves and others. They will enjoy getting to come up with their own kind expressions for others.

GRADES 6–12: For older students, it may be helpful to talk about how easy it is for us to be self-critical and put each other down. Opening up an initial conversation around why they think we are so mean to ourselves and each other might be very beneficial. It is especially useful to ask how they think this meanness affects us and our communities, and if they think we should keep things the way they are. It is incredibly helpful to get students on board with heartfulness instead of just telling them to be nice to each other.

FLOW AND TELL

Mindful listening is when we let go of our agendas and ideas to truly hear another person's perspective. We often have firm impressions of the people we like and the people we don't like. Learning to see beyond those judgments can be hard work, but it allows us to be more friendly and positive. The other part of mindful communication is mindful speaking, or speaking authentically. This means using our mindfulness to be aware of what is going on inside of us, and then being brave enough to share this with others. When we can really speak our truth and truly listen, true friendship and connection can thrive.

LEARNING OBJECTIVES

Empathy, emotional self-regulation, metacognition, focused attention, self-compassion, open-mindedness

Preparation and Considerations

This exercise works best when everyone is seated in a circle. Pass around a talking piece so that each student has a few chances to share his or her thoughts. If we break students into pairs, it's important that each pair is not too close to any of the others.

Speaking authentically can be an edgy experience for students. Insecurity can arise when youth speak with each other one on one. This practice should not be mandatory for any student who is uncomfortable with it.

Lesson

Let students know that today we will be learning how to communicate mindfully. Students will learn to communicate from the present moment instead of simply sharing past experiences or ideas about the future. Making a present-moment statement means simply stating what we experience right now in our bodies. We can say what sensations we feel in our bodies—what we see, hear, smell, or taste. We can also share our emotions—if we are, for instance, nervous, happy, or excited. Instead of Show and Tell we will be practicing Flow and Tell: sharing with each other whatever is flowing in our awareness right now.

Students begin by putting on their mindful bodies and practicing mindful listening for a minute, noticing everything they hear.

For one minute, they can scan through their bodies, noticing sensations.

For another minute, they can check into their emotions.

Then students can open up their awareness to perceive all of their sensations, breath, thoughts, and emotions at once.

Invite them to keep their eyes closed and continue to practice, and tell them that as they do this, they are going to learn how to speak mindfully. They will go around in a circle and, when it is their turn to speak, they can look inside and say what they are experiencing in the present moment.

We can start our sentence with "In the present moment I am aware of

_____ "

Some examples would be:

"In the present moment I am aware of an itch on my hand."
"In the present moment I'm aware of the sound of a truck."
"In the present moment I am aware of feeling nervous."
"In the present moment I am aware of my busy mind."

We can go around in a circle a few times, and everyone can share what they are experiencing in the present moment. Remind students to keep their eyes closed and their focus inside themselves. When students speak, remind them not to tell stories or describe ideas, but speak from what is happening right now. They can practice listening to other students without judgments or planning what they are going to say.

Dialogue Questions

Do you ever feel nervous or uncomfortable when you are talking to people?

Do you ever feel judged, or like you have to put on an act?

Inspiring Quote

“ *Be yourself; everyone else is already taken.* ”

—Oscar Wilde

Journaling Prompts

DRAWING: Draw a picture of what you feel like right now. Then show it to a classmate and tell him or her what your drawings are about. Ask your classmate to explain his or her drawing.

WRITING: Write about what you noticed in yourself as you were talking and listening.

Mindful Life Practice

Invite students to work on their mindful listening skills, really listening when someone is talking to them rather than simply waiting for their turn to talk. Students can, with intention, ask someone how they are doing and really try to listen mindfully. They may choose someone with whom they usually don't talk and try to get to know them by asking questions and listening to the responses.

Age and Stage

GRADES K–5: Students learn to speak from the present moment but sometimes need more explanation of the parameters. It can be helpful to begin by having kids share what they see, smell, and feel, going through all of the senses to illustrate what present moment senses are. Flow and tell can be a wonderful exercise to practice several times a day, inviting students into the present moment when they come into school, after transitions, or whenever there is a disturbance in the room.

GRADES 6–12: Students can really absorb these lessons to gain perspective on how they communicate with family, friends, and teachers. If there's time, the practice can begin in a circle and then break off into pairs, where students can practice speaking from the present moment. Many adolescents are grappling with the conflict between their deep desire to be authentic and real and a simultaneous and equally intense desire to fit in. This practice can be especially meaningful to students of this age, as it suggests they can be accepted exactly as they are and do not need to put on any masks.

ROSE AND THORN

When we bring our emotional intelligence into social interactions, we learn how to share our joys and our sorrows. Cultivating relationships and social environments in which we can be vulnerable and authentic helps us be ourselves and let go of stress. In this lesson, we learn to communicate authentically and listen mindfully. Listening mindfully necessitates that we pay close attention and reflect back what we have heard. This can create a real sense of connection and trust in a classroom.

LEARNING OBJECTIVES

Empathy, emotional self-regulation, metacognition, focused attention, stress reduction, cognitive flexibility, self-compassion, open-mindedness

Preparation and Considerations

Any time we are inviting students to share their emotions, we need to be sensitive to what may come up in the discussion. We want to make sure to talk to students about confidentiality and ask everyone to agree that whatever is shared will stay in the room. It is always important to remind students that they don't need to share and that they can always pass. If a student ever shares about abuse or something else that is outside the scope of the class, we can ask them to pause, let them know that what they are talking about is really important, and tell them that you want to talk to them about it after class. Make sure to have good collateral resources on hand.

Lesson

Ask students to begin by practicing some mindfulness of their emotions, simply sitting in their mindful bodies and checking in to see what is happening in their hearts. We can tell them to check the emotional weather patterns in their bodies, observing if they feel happy, stressed, angry, excited, or a mixture of feelings.

Tell students that we will be sharing what is happening in our lives with each other. We do this by telling one rose and one thorn. This means that we go around the circle and, when it is their turn, they can share one thing that has happened recently that they feel good about and one thing that they don't feel very good about. Remember to tell them they can always pass or choose to share only a rose or only a thorn.

As the instructor, we can start the exercise by sharing a rose and a thorn from our own lives. Remember to lead with something authentic but not overly emotional, demonstrating to students that they can share simple things—a rose could be getting to eat pizza, and a thorn could be not getting to eat ice cream.

After each person shares, another student can reflect back what they heard—by simply repeating the rose and the thorn, if they like.

Remember to have students pause at moments and see what it feels like to share what is happening for them and what it is like to listen.

Dialogue Questions

How do you usually feel about sharing thorns with people?

How does it feel before and after you share your thorn?

Inspiring Quote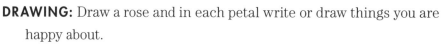

> **❝** *You open your heart knowing that there's a chance*
> *it may be broken one day and in opening your heart,*
> *you experience a love and joy that you never dreamed possible.* **❞**

—Bob Marley

Journaling Prompts

DRAWING: Draw a rose and in each petal write or draw things you are happy about.

WRITING: Write a list of one rose, one thorn, then another rose, then another thorn, and, as you keep alternating, see how you feel inside as you write them.

Mindful Life Practice

Ask students to find a person at home or at school who wants to share a rose and a thorn with them every day. Having a partner with whom they go back and forth every day provides an opportunity to practice and deepen their connections with others. This is a great practice for families to share around the dinner table as well.

Age and Stage

GRADES K–5: Younger students may need more examples of roses and thorns to understand the practice. It also may be necessary for instructors to mirror back each student's rose and thorn until they understand how to do this. Remind students to share only one rose and one thorn. If there are particularly chatty students we may want to use a timer or a bell to signify the end of each person's allotted time.

GRADES 6–12: For older students, this exercise can really help them learn how to share authentically and listen empathically. When they have some competency in the practice, we can have them pair off and practice together, sharing their roses and thorns and then having their partners reflect what they heard. This practice is also a wonderful opportunity to discuss vulnerability, authenticity, and friendship.

QUESTIONING ASSUMPTIONS

In this practice we bring our mental and emotional intelligence together to begin questioning our assumptions. Questioning assumptions helps us open our world-view, understand other perspectives, and develop empathy. Students can learn about their self-limiting beliefs and unconscious biases, and develop greater self-esteem and empathic esteem for others.

LEARNING OBJECTIVES

Empathy, executive functioning, emotional self-regulation, metacognition, focused attention, stress reduction, cognitive flexibility, self-compassion, open-mindedness

Preparation and Considerations

For this lesson we use everyday objects to help students examine their assumptions. Depending on the students, we may use a toy, a cell phone, or other objects that hold particular significance. Another way to teach this practice is to show some slides to the class with images that are particularly significant for students, such as a group of friends, two kids fighting, or a happy family.

Lesson

Ask the students to begin by putting on their mindful bodies and practicing popcorn thoughts for a minute. They can put a hand on their stomachs, feel their breath, and pop their hands up whenever a thought comes into their heads.

Then we can tell students that today we will be learning how to watch our popping thoughts in everyday life. We can explain how every one of us carries unconscious assumptions that can block us from truly understanding other people and things. Use the example of a time we might have tried a type of food, decided we didn't like it, and resolved to never try it again, even though our taste buds can change and foods we once hated can become our favorites.

Tell students to put on their mindful bodies but keep their eyes open to watch the objects or images we are going to show them. They may practice their mindful breathing as we place an object in front of them for a minute and invite them to notice what thoughts and assumptions pop into their heads as they examine it.

Next we ask what they noticed in their minds when they were looking at the object. It is important for us to demonstrate to students how associations with objects can vary widely from person to person.

Keep showing images or objects and ask students to notice how they respond to each one. Remind them to make note of their emotional responses to each object. Do they like the object or dislike it? Can they feel their bodies excited, tense, happy, or holding any other feeling in response to the object?

Finally, ask students to try looking at one more object without any thoughts or assumptions, simply observing the shapes and colors. Have them take a minute to think about their classmates and examine the assumptions that arise when they do. Invite students to take a fresh look at the people around them and question the assumptions they hold about them.

Dialogue Questions

Can you think of any other unconscious assumptions you hold?

What would it be like if you didn't have any assumptions?

Inspiring Quote

" *We don't see things as they are, we see them as we are.* "

—Anaïs Nin

Journaling Prompts

DRAWING: Draw things that you really like on one side of the page and things you don't like on the other side of the page.

WRITING: Write about one thing that you don't like and one thing that you do like. Ask yourself why you feel these ways about these things and write down what you notice.

Mindful Life Practice

Over the next day, students can try and notice their assumptions about the foods they usually like, the music they usually like, and the people they usually like, and see if they can question these assumptions. They can try and bring a fresh mind to their interactions.

Age and Stage

GRADES K–5: Younger students will need to be engaged with this practice in a fun way. Bring in fun toys, as well as things like broccoli or other objects they may not be as excited about. Instead of having students stare for a whole minute, ask them to look at the object for five seconds and then talk about how they feel about it. Even quickly showing the objects can produce great discussions about how they respond positively or negatively to various objects and how everyone responds differently.

GRADES 6–12: Older students can use the popcorn thoughts exercise and deepen it to observe how their minds pop with assumptions. Showing a slideshow of pictures of someone surfing, a stack of money, a town after an earthquake, and other evocative images can open up amazing discussions for students. It can be really beneficial to encourage discussions about racism and bias, demonstrating that everyone carries assumptions and how certain assumptions can create real problems.

MINDFUL ENGAGEMENT

This lesson is aimed at helping students integrate their mindfulness practice into their daily lives by having them teach these practices to each other. It is especially empowering for students to come up with ways to bring mindfulness into the world. They can bring their compassion, attention, and embodiment into the world as gifts for others.

> ### ■ LEARNING OBJECTIVES ■
> **Empathy, self-compassion, open-mindedness, contentment**

Preparation

Students will spend time in groups and will need their mindfulness journals. It is always important to be cognizant of cultural diversity within the class. Each student comes to the class with different resources and obstacles. When inviting students to create their mindfulness projects, be sensitive to each child's world.

Lesson

Talk to students about how we can be mindful in all aspects of our lives: when we are brushing our teeth, walking down the street, or talking with a friend. When we are mindful of the world, we begin to understand the people, animals, and environment all around us. With our heartfulness, we become empathic to the feelings and needs of others in our world. We can develop the motivation to help those in need.

Invite students into their mindful bodies and practice some mindful breathing. Then ask them to bring into their minds a moment when someone was really kind to them. This could involve, for example, a teacher or a friend, and could be a moment when someone gave them a gift, said something nice to them, or gave them a hug. Students can keep picturing this moment in their minds as if they were watching it on a TV screen. Ask them to notice how watching this scene makes them feel.

Now have students let the image go and this time imagine being nice to someone else. They might picture saying something nice to a friend or picking a flower and giving it to a teacher. They can picture doing a few kind acts in their minds and notice how this feels in their bodies. They can picture themselves as the most kind and giving person in the world and see what it feels like to be so generous.

Students then choose a commitment within themselves for their lives. They can share their commitments in pairs, with the whole group, or in their journals.

Dialogue Questions

What did it feel like when you imagined being nice to someone else?

What kind acts are you committed to doing in the world?

Inspiring Quote

66 The best way to find yourself is to lose yourself in the service of others. 99

—Mahatma Gandhi

Journaling Prompts

DRAWING: Draw a picture of yourself doing an act of kindness.

WRITING: Write your vision of how you can bring your mindfulness into the world.

Mindful Life Practice

Have students choose a mindfulness service project that will serve themselves and the community. Let them take some time to understand which qualities they have cultivated inwardly that they wish to share with the world. They might commit to visiting classes of younger students and teaching gratitude lessons or simply being nicer to their siblings. The mindful service work can be simple commitments of how they want to create positive changes in the world or real projects that they can do themselves or in a larger group.

Age and Stage

GRADES K–5: Students can visualize themselves being mindful in the world and then write or draw about it. They will have a fun time remembering moments when they did something kind for someone else and coming up with ideas of how they can be kind in the future. This is a good dialogue for strengthening their ability to respond in the future in ways they have already imagined.

GRADES 6–12: Students visualize how they would like to act in future situations and may have interesting conversations about why we often forget to be nice to each other. Students can plan ways to be mindful in their lives, and the whole class can even come up with a mindfulness project to complete together. Older students can be empowered by teaching mindfulness to younger students and choosing service projects to make a difference in the world.

Global
Literacy
Lessons

GLOBAL LITERACY

The air we breathe, the water we drink, the food we eat, the sun which makes everything grow, the land we stand upon, these are the gifts we are given every day, of which we are completely dependent on for our lives. With these practices, we help students understand their interdependence with the world. Using the skills from previous lessons, students will learn to see how their bodies, minds, and hearts are affected by their different environments. They will learn about their bodies, the objects around them, and the ecosystem they are part of. With this direct awareness students will be empowered to take care of their environment and to feel compassion for all living things.

MINDFUL EATING

When we eat mindfully, we gain a new way of relating to our world. Generally, we eat without bringing much awareness to the process. Our intention in this practice is to become aware of the great pleasure and beauty inherent in a normal daily experience.

This is by no means simply a practice of bringing awareness to taste. It is a full sense-based experience, during which we explore our sense of taste, touch, smell, hearing, and sight. The mindful eating practice helps us and our students bring full sensory awareness to everything in our lives, whether it is eating breakfast, playing sports, or hanging out with our friends.

LEARNING OBJECTIVES

Empathy, focused attention, open-mindedness, contentment

Preparation and Considerations

The ideal foods for this practice are small, tasty, and natural. A couple of raisins, an apricot, a tangerine, or other fruit will do. Chocolate or other candies may be distracting and make it harder for children to focus.

Be aware of any food allergies in the classroom. Some children may have very particular food preferences; you may need to bring an alternative snack. Remember to wash everyone's hands before beginning.

Lesson

It's nice to begin the mindful eating practice with a conversation about interconnectedness. Hold up the fruit and ask the students what it is. Where does it come from? Help students trace the food's path from the store back to the truck or ship on which it was delivered from the farm. Help them remember that the shopkeeper, the truck driver, and the farmer all played parts in delivering the fruit to us.

Have the students talk about what the fruit is made of. The seed, the water, the sun, and the soil have all contributed to the fruit in its current form. When they say that the raisin needs sunlight to grow, we can say, "So there must be sunshine in this raisin!" We may even talk about where this type of plant originated—was it Asia? South America? Africa? How did it get here?

Ask the students to get into their mindful bodies and take a few mindful breaths as we pass out the fruit. Once each student has some, invite them to open their eyes and examine it like mindful scientists, using their eyes to see every color and line as if they have never seen something like it before. Have them talk about what they see.

Invite the students to feel the fruit on their fingers as they roll it around. They can close their eyes and really focus on the touch of the fruit. Have them talk about what it feels like.

Have the students bring the fruit up close to their noses and give a good long smell. Ask them to talk about what it smells like.

Ask them if they have ever heard fruit make a sound. Have them put the fruit next to their ears and be very quiet while they rub it. Raisins will usually make a crinkling noise, while tangerines sound more slippery. They can talk about what they hear.

Finally, ask the students to hold their arms out, holding the fruit, and in slow motion bring the fruit toward their mouths and slowly touch it to their lips. Invite them to close their eyes and eat the fruit slowly, being aware of the texture on the tongue and teeth. Encourage them to be mindful enough to taste every moment.

Dialogue Questions

> What did you notice that you haven't noticed before?

> How would your life be different if you paid this much attention to everything?

Inspiring Quote

66 *To see the world in a grain of sand, and to see heaven in a wild flower, hold infinity in the palm of your hands, and eternity in an hour.* 99

—William Blake

Journaling Prompts

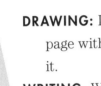

DRAWING: Draw a picture of the food you ate in the middle of a blank page with all of the elements and people that it needed to grow around it.

WRITING: Write down your favorite food, then describe all of the elements and people needed for that food to get to you.

Mindful Life Practice

Students can resolve to stop for at least a few breaths whenever they are eating, pausing to really appreciate their food (and improving digestion!). Students may want to choose one meal a day during which they slow down, appreciate their food, and think about all the elements that allowed it to reach them.

Age and Stage

GRADES K–5: Students enjoy the sensory experience of mindful eating, and younger kids love sharing what they smell, feel, see, hear, and taste. We can practice this game at snack time before the first bite. It's a wonderful way to get students to slow down and enjoy their food. Take time with each sensory exploration and remind younger children not to eat their raisins immediately when they receive them.

GRADES 6–12: Students can use this practice to attune to their senses and focus their attention. They can explore the most subtle sensations involved in eating, such as the mouth beginning to salivate even before they start eating and the way the mouth moves when it chews. This exercise can also support a science or history lesson about the origins of particular foods.

MINDFUL SPACES

When students become mindful of their inner worlds as well as the world around them, they can begin to understand the effect that different environments have on them. Understanding how we are affected by noises, lights, crowds, and other external phenomena is an incredibly empowering skill. Once students gain the capacity to understand the effects of the outside world on them, they can regulate themselves much better and make choices that will create greater balance in their lives.

LEARNING OBJECTIVES

Emotional self-regulation, metacognition, cognitive flexibility, open-mindedness, cognitive flexibility

Preparation and Considerations

This lesson requires some space changes. If you start the session in a classroom, move into the hall or head out to the playground if possible. If leaving the classroom is not possible, then shift the classroom environment by turning lights on and off, playing different types of music, and having kids sit in different arrangements. Consider clearly what your class will be able to do without getting too distracted or uncomfortable about being seen by their classmates. This lesson is used after students have already built a strong concentration practice as well as an understanding of their emotions and sensations.

Lesson

We can begin by inviting students to take a minute for an inside weather check of their sensations, thoughts, and emotions. Then they can check their outer world of sensations by focusing on the sounds around them. Invite students to be aware of the world all around them and the world inside them at the same time, seeing if they can notice the way the outer world affects their inner world.

Let the class know that we will be changing the spaces so that they can understand how a change of environment changes their inner worlds. Have them practice sitting mindfully as we turn off the lights in the room so they can see how this affects their minds, bodies, and hearts. Invite them to continue paying attention to their inner weather pattern as we turn on some soothing music. Then we may change the music to upbeat, funky music and have them notice how this affects them.

At the end of the session, have students notice what it is like when the lights are turned on. Invite them to continue noticing the changes in their minds, bodies, and hearts as they shift into sharing about the exercise. Encourage them to keep this mindful awareness even as they shift into the next subject.

Dialogue Questions

How did your inner weather pattern shift as the outside world changed?

What aspects of your experience didn't change when you shifted settings?

Inspiring Quote

66 You cannot step in the same river twice. 99

—Heraclitus

Journaling Prompts

DRAWING: Draw a picture of yourself in the middle of the page. Then draw all of the changing things that happen in a day around you.

WRITING: Make a list of things in your life that are always changing and another list of things that always stay the same.

Mindful Life Practice

Ask students to stay observant of their inner weather patterns after school and as they move through the day. Recommend that they monitor the literal weather patterns and notice how they feel inside when it is raining or sunny. They can reflect on how they feel when they wake up on a school day and how they feel when they wake up on the weekend. Invite students to investigate how different places, music, and even groups of people affect them.

Age and Stage

GRADES K–5: Younger students will enjoy this lesson when it is turned into a fun game. We can lead a short practice, asking them to notice their breath and after we make distinct changes to their environment, notice how the changes make them feel. We can play fun upbeat music and then relaxing ocean sounds, asking how the two make them feel. The practice of calling out a pause or asking them to notice their inner weather pattern can be used at any point of the day: for example, during a lesson, a game, or lunch.

GRADES 6–12: Students of this age group really begin to understand the effects of the outside world on their inner weather patterns. If it's possible to bring students outside of the classroom, we can have them bring their awareness to the ways these patterns are different in the classroom, in the hallways, on the playground, and even in the woods. This practice can start some amazing conversations for students to discuss the effects of different spaces and how they can take care of themselves in these various spaces.

NATURAL WORLD

One of the best ways to practice mindfulness is to be mindful in nature. The natural world has many teachings for us. Watching a tree can teach us a lot about stillness. Watching a hawk fly can help us understand focus. When we are disconnected from nature, we may forget that we are part of the web of life. If we become mindful about nature, we are much less likely to litter or do something harmful to the Earth: if we mindfully feel how we are part of the Earth, we will want to take care of it.

We can get in touch with the elements of nature within our own bodies. Even if there are no trees or animals around, we can explore nature in our own consciousness. Earth, fire, water, air, and space all have different effects on our bodies. A natural word practice helps kids feel their solidity, creativity, calmness, flow, and spaciousness.

LEARNING OBJECTIVES

Executive functioning, emotional self-regulation, focused attention, stress reduction, open-mindedness, contentment, cognitive flexibility

Preparation and Considerations

If we have access to nature trails or a garden it can be wonderful to bring students to a natural space. There we give them time to sit and listen to the sounds, smell the smells and see the beautiful colors. It is ideal to do this practice outdoors, but possible to do it inside. We can bring pictures of the five elements to class, or literally bring water and earth to give children a visual and visceral image. It is useful to point out the elements that surround us: the sun as fire, ocean as water, ground as earth, breeze as air, and the space that permeates all things.

Lesson

Tell students that they can learn a lot from the elements of nature. Earth, fire, water, and air are four elements we see in the world, and we also feel them in our bodies. In this mindfulness lesson, we become aware of what these four sensations feel like within the body. We will also build our awareness of a fifth element: space.

Invite students to sit tall while letting their bodies relax and focusing on their breath. Remind them that with every inhale, we breathe in the oxygen the trees have breathed out. With every exhale of carbon dioxide, the trees are thanking us as they take it in.

Now have them bring to mind the image of a mountain and feel as if they are equally strong and solid. With each breath, they can feel more solid on the Earth, sensing the earth elements in their bodies.

Now have them bring to mind the image of a still lake and feel as if they are equally calm. With every breath, they can imagine being smooth and serene like the water element.

Now they bring to mind an image of the sun and feel as if their bodies are shining in all directions. With every breath, they can feel as if their bodies are shining like the element of fire.

Next they bring to mind the image of leaves shaking in the wind and notice all the different sensations moving around their bodies. With every breath, they can notice the constantly shifting sensations of the wind element.

Finally, they imagine themselves floating in outer space and getting the feeling that there is nothing around them. With every breath, they feel as if they are floating and feeling the element of space.

Now they become aware of the room around them and feel themselves sitting on the ground. When they are ready, have them slowly open their eyes.

Dialogue Questions

What was your favorite element and how did it feel?

What are the elements that make up a pencil?

Inspiring Quote

— —

" When one tugs at a single thing in Nature, he finds it attached to the rest of the world. "

—John Muir

— —

Journaling Prompts

DRAWING: Draw a picture of yourself as your favorite element.

WRITING: Write a few adjectives describing how each element felt.

Mindful Life Practice

Encourage students to find a quiet place in nature, or just next to a plant, and sit there silently. They can open their senses deeply to what the natural world has to say. This is their sit spot, and they can go to this place whenever they want to relax and be mindful. They can go there every day, even if it's just for a minute, and listen to nature.

Age and Stage

GRADES K–5: Students love to do this elemental practice. It is helpful to use visuals and have them really engage imaginatively with the idea of being a mountain. We can have young kids picturing themselves as all types of animals and natural elements, seeing how this makes them feel.

Imagining that they are little mice often makes them feel safe, and imagining that they are lions makes them feel strong.

Field trips in nature also make wonderful outings. Kids love to make lists of things to identify or find different kinds of flowers or trees, different colors, or different sounds, checking the things off a list as they find them. Engaging students with the natural world is interactive, rather than one-directional learning with a textbook or computer. Nature can be an incredible interactive teacher.

GRADES 6–12: Students can use this practice to notice the different aspects of their awareness. We can teach them about biology and look at the actual elements active in their bodies, spending some time leading them in noticing the ways these different elements feel. Older students can learn how quickly they can shift their state of mind by using different elements: becoming more grounded with earth, flexible with water, energized by fire.

KNOW YOUR WORLD

Mindfulness opens up a curiosity that can help us understand how we are connected with the world. In this practice we help students inquire into their world in ways they might not have thought to do. We can help students to understand their connection to the local environment, history, and culture. This helps students develop compassion for others and the natural world. This also helps them orient to place and feel more empowered.

LEARNING OBJECTIVES

Empathy, metacognition, focused attention, open-mindedness

Preparation and Considerations

To help students inquire into the world around them, we begin by inquiring into ourselves. Once we have decided on a list of questions to ask students, we can pose the questions to ourselves before leading the class. Think of the diversity of the class before choosing the questions, so that everyone will feel included.

Lesson

Begin with a short practice in which students put on their mindful bodies and notice their breath, their physical sensations, and everything else that is happening on the inside. They shift their awareness to sounds, smells, and everything else on the outside. They shift between inside awareness and outside awareness a few times and then try to be aware of the inside and the outside at once.

Let students know that today we will open our minds to try to be mindful of what is happening around us. Ask the students a few of the questions below and see if they come up with answers. If not, share what you know with the students.

Next offer a list of questions to the students for them to work on in small groups or by themselves.

What direction are you facing right now? (North, East, South, West)

What is the ground you are on made of?

Where is the moon in its cycle right now?

If you turn on the water in the sink, where is it coming from?

Where does the electricity in the lights in this room come from?

If you throw something in the garbage, where does it go?

What is the history of this school?

Who lived on this land 1,000 years ago, and what was their life like?

Where do your ancestors come from?

What type of climate do you live in?

Dialogue Questions

What other questions do you have about your world?

How might you act differently after finding out where your electricity and water come from and where your garbage goes?

Inspiring Quote

66 *Our task must be to free ourselves by widening our circle of compassion to embrace all living creatures and the whole of nature and its beauty.* 99

—Albert Einstein

Journaling Prompts

DRAWING: Draw a picture of water from the sink and the pipes that bring it there going all the way back to the lake or reservoir it comes from.

WRITING: Write down a list of questions you have about your world, such as who built your school or what and where is the closest river.

Mindful Life Practice

Ask students to get interested in their worlds. Have them choose some things to learn about and go to the library or ask people in the community who can help them learn about their worlds. Then they come back to class and share with each other what they have found.

Age and Stage

GRADES K–5: Younger students may not know many answers to the questions we ask. Share the information through fun stories of how the rain falls, collects in reservoirs, and is piped into the school or about the sanitation workers who take the garbage to giant garbage centers and landfills. Tell students about our world and then continue to ask them questions, so that they build up an understanding of where they are.

GRADES 6–12: Adolescents and young adults can really run with this practice. We help students ask questions about their world and then support them in understanding how they feel about the way things are. If students realize that their garbage is sent in barges out to the ocean, they can consider their actions more closely and even work together on a recycling campaign. By getting children to understand their world, we help them appreciate their surroundings, as well as find things they want to change.

LIFE CYCLE ASSESSMENT

Being mindful helps us know our bodies, minds, and hearts. It also helps us understand the world around us, the communities of people that populate it, and the natural world. We can look with eyes of compassion and focus at the people, animals, foods, and objects in our world and try to understand their origins. When we understand where things come from, we gain a deeper relationship with our world and the choices we make about how to live.

LEARNING OBJECTIVES

Empathy, executive functioning, focused attention, self-compassion, open-mindedness, cognitive flexibility

Preparation and Considerations

We can explore the origins of anything but it is important to begin with simple and natural objects, such as leaves or stones. Then we can move up in complexity to manufactured objects, like a pencil or a spoon. Explore whatever we already have in the room. Have these objects ready for the lesson, and do a little research into their life cycles.

We can also research the origins of our school and region, the building we are in, and the land we are on so that we begin the class with an explanation of the origins of the place we are in.

Lesson

Open the lesson by telling students that we will learn about where things come from. We use mindfulness to look into the origins of things and understand their life cycles. A good way to describe what we mean is by telling students about the origins of the building we are in and some history of the land we are on.

Pass out natural objects, such as pebbles, acorns, shells, or any other small object students can hold in their hands. They can sit mindfully with the object in their hands and practice a few mindful breaths. They take a minute to really feel all the textures of the object, keeping their eyes closed. Then they open their eyes and look closely at the object, really examining its colors and shapes. Next they can smell the object and see if it has any smell. They can even listen to it by tapping or shaking it.

Ask the students to figure out the life cycle of this object together. Where did it come from? What elements conspired for it to become what it is? What might happen to it next?

When the students have done their first assessment, we can move them on to more complex explorations. Ask them to pick up one simple manufactured object, such as a crayon or a ruler. After examining it thoroughly with their senses, as they did with the first object, they can try to figure out what the object is made of. Once they think they have figured out the components, they can figure out the life cycle of the materials that made it. Once they have explored where the materials came from, they can figure out how the object was made and how it ended up here. They can also postulate what will happen to it and its materials next.

A further step would be to help students track their carbon footprint from the resources they use. They can also track their handprint, which is the amount of environmentally conscious choices they can make to offset their footprint.

Dialogue Questions

How hard would it be to answer these questions with an object like a computer?

How do you feel toward the objects now, after this exploration?

Inspiring Quote

66 *A society grows great when old men plant trees whose shade they know they shall never sit in.* 99

—Greek proverb

Journaling Prompts

DRAWING: Draw a picture with a natural object in the middle and a circle around it. On the circle, draw the different ways this object has looked before and might look later.

WRITING: Write down the life cycle, past and future, of an object you can see from where you are.

Mindful Life Practice

Ask students to find an object where they live and figure out its life cycle. They can research the different materials and where they were sourced. Have them find out how long it takes for these materials to decompose. A full life cycle assessment can be an amazing study.

Age and Stage

GRADES K–5: Students will be interested in the sensory experience of the different objects. We can have them close their eyes and try to guess what the objects are by feeling, smelling, and listening. Students may enjoy coming up with the past and the future of the object. It can also be helpful to turn this into a story about a tree or a shell and how it grew up and lived its life. Younger students may have a harder time understanding the many components and tracking the history of a pencil, but turning this into a story about the tree and the lead and how the factory put them together can be fun for them.

GRADES 6–12: Students can use this practice to learn many academic lessons. Science, math, history, current events, and many other realms of learning can be explored here. When students track the sources of different metals and oil-based products, they will learn a lot of information, sometimes difficult to hear, about where things are mined and the workers who make the goods.

Integration
Practices

The following practices can be woven throughout the school day. These are practices that use the foundations of the five mindful literacies and help students be mindful in everything they do. Here we explore some creative ways to lead practices focusing on themes such as stress, test taking, and empowering students to lead their own lessons. These examples show us how to create our own mindfulness lessons around various academic and social-emotional topics. These are called integration practices because they are meant to be integrated into the school day and also because they help students integrate all of the information and transformation they have received.

WEATHER REPORT

Once students know the five realms of mindful literacy, we bring them all together. At moments throughout the day, we can have students check in to their bodies, minds, hearts, relationships, and environments. They learn to rapidly become aware of the state of their inner and outer worlds. This capacity to reflect on all aspects of our awareness simultaneously is an amazing tool for regulation, attention, and prosocial behavior.

Invite the students to begin by checking in to their bodies. Tell them that it's like they are checking the weather report and noticing where the sensations are and what they are like. We want to be able to look at the sensations and energy in the body without preferring one sensation over another. We simply scan through our bodies for a minute, noticing what is there.

Then we explore the realm of the mind. We check into the weather pattern of our thoughts and mind states. Invite students to see how focused they are, how busy their thoughts are, and generally what the state of their minds are. They can watch thoughts move by like clouds.

Then students can check into their hearts. Have them look at the weather pattern of their emotions. Without trying to change their emotions, have them see if they can accept whatever they find inside. Challenge them to notice what emotions are present, their stress levels, and how open their hearts are.

Then students check into the weather patterns of relationships. Have them reflect on the current dynamics in the classroom and in relationships with other students and teachers. They simply take a moment to see how much drama or friendliness is happening. They can reflect on their own levels of empathy, anger, or other emotions.

Now students can look into the weather patterns of the world around them. This can mean experiencing the physical temperature, visual sur-roundings, and outside sounds. Students can open their awareness as wide as they can, seeing if they notice the actual weather patterns that their bodies are within.

Finally students can sit back as if they are in movie theater seats expe-riencing all five realms simultaneously. It's as if they are opening the view 360 degrees to be aware of everything all at once. The more they practice this, the better they will be able to drop into a relaxed state of mindful presence.

We can have students move through the practice at different speeds depending on their age. With younger kids we may play with them in expe-riencing each realm for about 15 seconds. Older students could deeply experience each realm for at least a minute. This practice is best done regularly, having students open every day with it or doing a five-minute weather check a few times throughout the day.

STRESS CHECK

Here we offer students a way to track their stress levels. Instead of needing to regulate our students once they have exploded with stress, we can teach them to catch themselves before they reach their boiling point. Then students can regulate themselves using mindfulness practices or asking for help when they realize they are reaching a maximum stress point.

Students should gauge where they are on a 10-point stress scale, 1 being chill and 10 being boiling. We can show students the image of a thermometer so they can see how at the bottom the temperature is cool and up top it is hot. Explain how when we check into our emotions, we can feel how sometimes they are calm down around 1 to 3 and when they are really stressed they pop up around 7 to 10.

Explain to students how a little bit of stress is important for us to get anything done. The realm between four and six is an optimal zone when we are taking a test or working hard on a project.

Have students practice relaxing every bone and muscle in their bodies and see how low they can get their stress level. Then have them think about the hardest test they have ever taken and see how high their stress level goes. Finally invite them to try and find a balanced stress zone where they are relaxed and at the same time very focused.

We can use this scale regularly with students to ask them where they are on the stress level when we notice them heating up. Explain that when they are reaching up to seven or higher we want them to practice some calming breaths or let us know so we can support them.

We may also ask the whole class what they think the group stress level is. With this we can take the temperature of the room; when the class seems too hot, we can invite everyone to take some calming breaths together.

MINDFUL TEST PREP

Students can feel very anxious around test taking, performance, and a variety of other experiences. Of course we want to support them so they don't have to feel the discomfort of stress. It also will help them perform better if they are relaxed and confident.

Invite students to remember the hardest test or stressful competition they have ever experienced. It is helpful to have them imagine the scene, the colors of the room, the people around them, and other details so they really reconnect to it. Then ask them to scan through their bodies and see what stress comes when they put themselves back in that moment and where they are on the stress scale.

Once students have experienced the stress from the old experience, have them take a few vacuum breaths until they feel more relaxed. Then have them imagine they are going back to the test or competition with calm and confidence. They can picture themselves acing the test or performing their piano recital to perfection.

Another way to help students drop stress quickly is to have them once again imagine a difficult test. Have them pick up a pen or other simple object in their hand and hold it tightly. As they picture the stressful event, they put all their stress into squeezing that pen. As they hold onto it, they take a few vacuum breaths. When they are ready, they say to themselves "I'm letting go of my stress." As they say this, they open their hand, letting the object drop and letting their whole body relax.

These practices can be used before a test, a field trip, or any other time we notice the stress in the class rising. Students can be encouraged to use this practice themselves in the middle of a test or when they notice their stress levels rising. Remind them that even though this may take 10 seconds in the middle of a test, it will help them be more confident and present for the rest of the time.

WHO'S DRIVING?

A powerful concept for students is to explain that we all have many parts within us. We have a scared part of ourselves, a silly prankster part, a serious part, and many other inner characters. It's good to give a lot of examples to help them understand what we mean by "parts." We can go through a list and have the students close their eyes and see if they identify with each character and see what these parts feel like inside. A wonderful example is from the movie *Inside Out*. We could talk about each of the emotions of joy, sadness, disgust, fear, and anger. We can use examples of animals or characters that portray courage, kindness, impulsivity, calmness, and other personality traits. Have the students tell us what it feels like in their bodies when they are in touch with these parts.

Invite students to write a list of all their parts and describe what each is like. Or they can draw pictures of all of the different aspects of themselves. Once they have a feel for all of the different aspects of themselves, we can introduce them to the idea that there is another part of them that can be compassionate and aware of all the parts—their mindful part. Have the students think of all of the different parts inside themselves and witness them with compassion and acceptance.

Explain to students how sometimes having so many parts is like driving a car with all these different characters inside. The problem is that sometimes we let the angry part take the wheel. This is when we act out and do something we wished we hadn't done. What we can do with mindfulness is put the angry part of ourselves safely in the back and have the mindful part take the wheel. We don't kick any parts out of the car; we simply give them a comfortable spot in the back and let the mindful part do the driving. If a scared or angry part has something to say, we want to listen to them, because sometimes they have important information, but we don't just hand over the wheel.

We can invite kids to witness all of their parts throughout the day and come back to discuss what they find. We especially want them to see if they notice when different parts try to grab the wheel and whether their mindful part can gain control.

WHO WANTS TO LEAD A LESSON?

A wonderful way to empower students and engage them in mindfulness is to have them teach the practices. Begin by letting students know they will be learning how to teach mindfulness. Then ask them who thinks they could lead a mindful breathing practice for the rest of the class.

When someone volunteers, ask if they need any help or if they want to try it themselves. We can always offer some wording for them to use.

Next ask who wants to lead a mindful listening practice, a mindful movement practice, or any other recommendations. Then ask students if they want to lead any other mindfulness practices they can think of.

Students sometimes come up with some fascinatingly creative practices. Usually it is beneficial to support them in being creative with this unless they are leading to something that seems way off base.

From this point we can invite students to teach these practices to other people in their community. We strengthen their teaching skills by having them regularly leading lessons for each other in class and developing fun new ways to focus and relax.

PART IV

Recommendations for Integration

"I have been teaching my mom a lot of mindfulness because she gets mad a lot. I say, 'You seem a little angry. Do you want to do some mindfulness with me?' and she always answers yes and then she's happy."
—THIRD-GRADE STUDENT, SAN FRANCISCO

Eventually the ideal of mindful education is to seamlessly integrate the practices into the school environment. Once the students have learned the basic literacies of their bodies, minds, hearts, society, and world, they become fluent in mindfully bringing these into their whole lives. Here we explore some ways that mindfulness can be woven into the everyday classroom experience. Without needing to stop and take time for a lesson, mindfulness can become a foundation for all learning and teaching. The following are recommendations of how to incorporate mindfulness into our work with students.

A DAY IN THE LIFE OF A MINDFUL CLASS

Mindful Moments

Scheduling mindful moments during the day is conducive to group cohesion and will help everyone feel safer and more attentive. Start class with a short practice of mindful listening, belly breathing, or deep relaxation. The flow and tell practice is a great way to start as well, bringing everyone into the present moment and connecting with each other. It can be beneficial to simply have a period of time in the beginning of the day where students sit silently, practicing however they want. Eventually you could choose a student to open the class by leading a mindfulness practice. This is empowering for the students and a great way to get everyone invested.

Early on, students may only feel comfortable sitting silently for 30 seconds, but eventually we may be able to build up to five minutes or more. We can start and end every day with a little practice and find a time at least once to practice in the middle of the day. Scheduled around transitions, mindfulness practices can be very helpful in bringing students back to a place of stillness. If the whole school, students, teachers, and all, can meet together to sit silently or have a mindful school meeting, so much the better.

Time In

Teachers and students can learn to ask for a "time in" when there is a lot of commotion in class or when an emotional experience has arisen, such as a disagreement or a fight between students. Instead of a "time out," this is an

223

opportunity for the class to collectively notice what is happening and find regulation together.

Teachers can model this practice when we find the class growing dysregulated and calling a "time in" by saying something like, "I'm noticing that there is a lot of chaos in the room right now. Can we all take a moment to notice what it feels like in the room?" It is also important to empower students to call for a time in when they feel like the class needs a moment of reflection. This is a perfect time to practice some vacuum breaths and have students build their emotional regulation skills.

Mindful Reminders

We can create reminders for ourselves and students to support a mindful environment. We can ask students to take three deep breaths any time they hear a bell, when the intercom goes on, or at some other everyday cue. Students may remember to focus on specific moments such as their mindful steps as they are walking to lunch or to focus on the first and last bites of a meal. We can put up reminders around our rooms that remind them of things like being in the present moment or breathing to invite them back to mindfulness.

Students can also begin to think of the distraction game as something that is happening all the time. Have them try to notice when they get distracted by the door opening, by students making noises, or any other attention-grabber they can use to build their attention muscles. Students can notice when they have assumptions and try to do acts of kindness. We help them realize that the mindfulness lessons we explore are a way of life.

Chill Space

A chill space is somewhere in a classroom or other room in the school dedicated to helping students feel safe and nurtured. It is best if the space is collaboratively created with the students. Examples of what would be in the space are things like tactile objects to play with, coloring materials, or soothing music on a music player. The space can be decorated with pillows, fabric, and natural things.

Students are self-referred to this space. This is not a spot that a teacher sends the students; youth can go there when they want. They go to the space when they are feeling dysregulated, and they come back out when they are ready to learn. Most teachers find that students go to the space right before they would usually act out and they don't stay in for too long.

Some schools use the corner of their rooms as a "peace corner." Others have a whole room where there is a mindfulness teacher or counselor who creates a space for the student to de-stress and regulate.

Using Mindfulness Language

Building a mindfulness vocabulary will help students speak articulately about their inner lives and will give the community a common language. As we develop attention, empathy, and regulation, we can adopt the following language so teachers, students, administrators, and parents can be on the same page. Principals can make announcements reminding students to take some vacuum breaths before the big tests if they get nervous, or they can read a few notes of gratitude written by students. The following is a list of words that can be introduced as themes and definitions of the main concepts we are working with in our mindfulness lessons.

AMYGDALA: A structure in the brain associated with emotions, fear, and aggression. We can explain to students how mindfulness can help us to relax the amygdala to limit our reactivity.

ASSUMPTIONS: A thought that is assumed to be true without proof. With mindfulness we look more deeply at our assumptions and gain a clearer understanding of ourselves and of those around us.

CAUSE AND EFFECT: The relationship between events in which one is the result of the other. We teach students how they are affected by the world around them and how they affect the world with their actions.

DISTRACTION: That which keeps the mind from being able to maintain focus. By witnessing distractions students build their ability to maintain attention.

EMOTIONAL INTELLIGENCE: The capacity to be aware of one's emotions and to navigate relationships with discernment and empathy. We want to teach students that emotional intelligence is as important as the intelligence we use for mathematics and memorization.

EMOTIONAL REGULATION: The ability to respond to and care for the emotions and feelings regularly arising within us. Whether the emotion is joy or grief, students learn to be fully present with the feelings without falling out of balance.

EMPATHY: The capacity to understand and care for the feelings of others. Instead of simply telling students to be nice to each other we teach them how to experience what is happening in another's heart.

FOCUS: The capacity to maintain attention on a chosen object. We can help students to build their attention muscles by using various focusing practices.

FOOTPRINT: The impact of a person or society on the environment. Together with students we can learn about our ecological impact, facing some difficult truths about how we affect the Earth.

GRATITUDE: The quality of appreciation and the readiness to express thankfulness in return. We can create a culture of gratitude by having it as a major theme in our classrooms.

HANDPRINT: Representation of the positive impact we have on the environment. With this concept we can learn how to diminish our negative environmental impact, empowering students to live more consciously.

IMPULSIVITY: Displaying behavior categorized by reactivity and little forethought. Students can become familiar with how impulses feel in their bodies, empowering them with nonreactivity and self-reflection.

INTERCONNECTION: Understanding how everything is linked up in a web of relationships. If we look deeply enough we see how every person and thing is mutually dependent on one another.

NEOCORTEX: A brain region associated with executive functioning and believed to be the most recently evolved part of the brain. We give students an understanding of how to support this brain region to succeed in their tasks.

ORIGINS: Looking deeply to find where something comes from. Whether it is a pencil or our own ancestry we can inquire to learn how and where something began.

RELAXATION: A state of being calm, tranquil, and free from tension and stress. The ability to relax is a precursor to being able to learn well and therefore a most foundational skill.

STRESS: A state of social, emotional, or mental tension. We teach students the ability to name the stress levels they feel in their bodies as well as noticing the tension levels around them.

Best Practices

From the lessons we have explored, there are some that are easily adapted to short offerings. Ringing a bell and having students listen until they can't hear it or taking a few vacuum cleaner breaths can take less than 30 seconds. Here are some of the go-to lessons to use in the midst of class.

> **WEATHER REPORT:** At many moments throughout the day we can call out a weather report to see what students are experiencing in their minds, bodies, hearts, and in the world around them. This helps students to build their ongoing mindful awareness.

> **STRESS TEST:** We can regularly invite students to check-in with their bodies and see where their stress levels are. The more we introduce them to their stress levels the more they will be able to track their own stress and regulate themselves.

> **SHAKE STILL:** If there is a lot of energy in the room, letting students shake and then freeze is a great way to bring in some awareness. This is a great exercise to use around transitions and whenever the room is chaotic.

> **DEEP RELAXATION:** Giving students an opportunity to relax and be still is an amazing gift. After transitioning from the playground, before a test, or right when students arrive at school, students can use this technique to settle in their bodies.

> **ANIMAL MOVES:** Some fun breathing movements are a good way to help students connect to their bodies in a mindful way. When students need a break from thinking, these stretching movements are a great option, and students usually enjoy coming up with their own moves.

> **ANCHOR BREATH:** Returning to the breath again and again supports attention and emotional regulation. This is a foundational mindfulness practice to remind students to repeat many times throughout the day.

> **MINDFUL LISTENING:** The simple practice of listening to a long resounding sound is a wonderful way to focus together. This becomes a great way to begin and end classes. This is a short and clear way to attune the senses.

> **VACUUM BREATH:** Whenever there is a conflict or stress in the room, it can be incredibly beneficial to ask students to notice what is happening in their bodies and then take a few vacuum cleaner breaths.

> **GENERATING GRATITUDE:** Even a short practice of generating gratitude can help students connect to their hearts and feel happy. Students can begin or end the day going around in a circle and sharing their gratitude. Whenever the class seems in the doldrums, this exercise can bring a breath of fresh air.

> **FLOW AND TELL:** This is a wonderful way to bring the class together to communicate what's happening for each of them in the present moment. This is a great way to start and end the day.

> **POPCORN THOUGHTS:** This practice helps develop the capacity to witness the way thoughts are arising in the mind. When the class is distracted or before a test this is a great way to remind the class how to stay focused.

Mindful Mathematics

There are so many creative ways to integrate mindfulness into math, science, language, and other classes. The first trick is simply to ask students to notice what's going on inside them during the lessons. They learn to say when they are feeling stressed or distracted, or if their bodies need to move. During testing times and other intense attention moments, we might have students practice some vacuum breaths or attention builders.

We can also offer mindful science lessons, where students use their focused eyes to be observant scientists. We can use literature and stories to reflect on the mindfulness themes like self-awareness and kindness.

Students may learn how to focus in math class so that as they are focusing on a theorem, they can let all the mental chatter float past. It is so important when discussing current events to help students feel their social and emotional connection to what's happening in the world.

MINDFUL EDUCATION LESSON WORKSHEET

When introducing a new mindfulness lesson to students, you can put together a lesson plan tailored for your particular class. Depending on the demographic of students, you will have to adapt the content and make it accessible. It is also great to bring in your own expertise and fun ways of teaching. You can teach mindfulness through art, storytelling, or other creative avenues. Here we have a chance to create a lesson plan from a template. This is a good way to recognize what the intentions and learning objectives are for leading the practice and how to successfully impart mindfulness tools.

MINDFUL EDUCATION LESSON

1 Begin by writing the intention. What is the hoped-for outcome of offering this lesson?

_____
_____
_____

2 Choose an activity from the curriculum section to begin with as a template to adapt and write why this lesson is of interest.

_____
_____
_____

3 Name one or more learning objective this lesson hopes to foster.

_____
_____
_____
_____

4 Write some ways to make this lesson accessible to the particular group that will be receiving it.

_____
_____
_____

5 Write a few sentences about what will happen in the following steps of the lesson sequence.

- Opening Mindful Moment

_____
_____

- Check-In and Report Back

_____
_____

- New Lesson Introduction

_____
_____

- Experiential Practice

_____
_____

- Sharing/Dialogue

_____
_____

- Integration/Journaling

_____
_____

- Mindful Life Practice

_____
_____

- Closing Mindful Moment

_____
_____

6 Reflect on how it was to put this lesson together.

_____
_____
_____

INTRODUCING MINDFULNESS TO OUR COMMUNITIES

Here we address how to stimulate interest in mindfulness for educators. We explore how buy-in necessitates an interest in the personal benefits that these modalities offer educators themselves instead of simply wanting to offer the practices to their students. To cultivate personal interest in mindfulness, we must inspire introspection, which means that the educators will be looking at their own emotions, mind-sets, and behaviors. Looking inside in this way offers the opportunity for finding greater meaning in our lives, letting go of stress, cultivating joy, and so many other benefits. Before reaping the benefits, however, we often must face vulnerabilities in our lives that we have not been paying attention to. We explore how to work skillfully and empathically with resistance in individuals as well as systemic "stuckness." We show how to inspire educators to find their own intrinsic motivation for personal well-being and self-care.

Recommendations

START WITH THE HEART

We begin by welcoming educators to understand that mindfulness is important for their own well-being. When these practices are seen as just another intervention to be imposed on the students, they will never generate the changes that are possible when a whole community commits to developing presence and compassion together. Therefore we must explain clearly why mindfulness for the adults is an endeavor worth our educators' and school's time and energy.

BENEFITS OF MINDFULNESS

It is helpful to begin by laying out the value of mindfulness and connecting the direct ways these practices can enhance people's lives. The benefits are physical, emotional, psychological, and social. There are so many relevant examples for how mindfulness can support our lives. The best examples to share with colleagues are those that we have personally experienced. We share how mindfulness has helped us focus, be more compassionate with kids, or any other genuine transformation we have experienced from our practice. Write up a list of anecdotes and your personally experienced benefits from mindfulness practice so we can offer these to colleagues. Using small, specific, significant examples can be more effective than just preaching the benefits.

THE SCIENCE

The science of mindfulness is evolving by the day. When talking to colleagues, have some research and scientifically backed anecdotes on hand of how mindfulness benefits attention, emotional regulation, compassion, and other factors pertinent to the particular audience. We can use these when we give a talk or even when chatting with a fellow teacher. Educators will be moved by hearing how mindfulness might raise test scores as well as how it decreases stress and burnout for teachers. Explaining the neurological benefits of the practices can be particularly impressive.

SELF-CARE AND WELL-BEING

I have never been to a school where the teachers said they had too much time. With the profound amount of tasks and responsibilities in a teacher's day, stress exacerbates the feeling that there is never enough time. Framing mindfulness as an opportunity to slow down and focus on self-care and well-being is a great way to appeal to teachers. Frame the benefits of mindfulness with language and descriptions that educators will easily understand. Everyone will nod their heads when we ask about burnout, stress, and feeling out of balance. We can explain mindfulness as a way to take care of ourselves, find balance, de-stress, and cultivate well-being.

WHAT HURTS?

When speaking to colleagues, begin with the universal human struggles that mindfulness and emotional intelligence address. Everyone can relate to wanting less stress and more happiness. Schools can connect around common difficult themes such as community drama, stressed schedules, and burnout. Finding stress themes for educators can be a really helpful way to bring a community together. Being able to name what we are struggling with, without projecting blame, gives perspective and the empowerment to use mindfulness for resolution.

AUDIENCE ENGAGEMENT

Everyone wants to be happy and not to be stressed. We can find each person's language for this. What are each person's stressors and hopes? Use metaphors related to football, music, nature, or whatever the group will resonate with. Nelson Mandela made allies with his former adversaries by learning their greatest interest (rugby), and then connected and unified a nation by finding a common cause. What do your colleagues care about and what do they struggle with? Use mindful attention and attunement to see how mindfulness practices can be helpful.

FINDING COMMONALITY

What would everyone like doing together that brings them into the present moment, in their bodies, hearts, and community? It could be dancing, hiking, or singing together. Ask them, "What do you do that helps you feel more alive and present?" Mindfulness doesn't need to mean closing our eyes and sitting quietly. It's important to help a school community learn how to connect in a way that is nonwork, nontechnological, noncompetitive, and pro-presence. Bringing a school community out of a competitive and stressed atmosphere into a cooperative and relaxed space is incredibly helpful.

THE DIRECT EFFECT

When presenting mindfulness, offer some direct exercises that exemplify the benefits of the practices. Offer a relaxation practice, a focusing practice, a kindness practice, and any other exercises colleagues will resonate with. Help them see the busyness of their minds and then offer a quick mind-calming practice or invite them to notice the stress in their bodies and then do a progressive relaxation exercise. It's very important to give them a visceral experience of how mindfulness can be helpful.

FIND MINDFULNESS CHEERLEADERS

Instances where mindfulness is successfully integrated into schools are fueled by groups of dedicated practitioners. If a principal or administrator is really on board, it is obviously helpful, but a small group of teachers, parents, and community can create an amazing movement. Trying to do this work all on our own can feel isolating. Of course it is fine to simply offer mindfulness in our own classroom, but having a community that we can meet with regularly to talk about what's working and what's not is very supportive.

Precautions

NO NEW AGE LINGO

With mindfulness, we are talking about very important things, such as how to find greater meaning in our lives, balance, and contentment. We need to talk about these in a universal way with a scientific and practical base. We can ask questions like,

> "Would you like a greater capacity to focus and have less distraction?"
> "Would you like to be less stressed and more balanced in your life?"
> "Would you like more happiness and contentment in your life?"

We can ask these kinds of questions with psychologically grounded and scientific validity. We speak to these very human aspects of life in a way that will resonate with everyone. Remember not to use words that have religious or culturally specific language that may alienate people. Words such as *stress*, *happiness*, *attention*, *resilience*, and *well-being* are all we need.

CAN'T PUSH THE RIVER

Everyone loves a mindfulness practitioner, but no one wants a mindfulness preacher. Remember that the greatest mindfulness teaching comes from our embodiment of kind and attentive presence. Most successful introductions of mindfulness in schools come from one teacher quietly integrating the practices in their classroom. The surrounding classroom teachers see the amazing, relaxed, and empathic students and want to know the secret. This can build into a movement in the school. The opposite can be true if we are seen as proselytizers trying to force a new curriculum on the school. Even though it comes from great intentions, pushing mindfulness may close many people down, and then there will be more resistance later.

NOT ANOTHER CURRICULUM

The last thing many schools want is one more curriculum. It is important to frame mindfulness not as another curriculum teachers and administrators have to buy into. Mindfulness can be integrated into any class, any school, and any curriculum. In the same way that stretching and physical training are necessary for every sport, mindfulness and emotional intelligence are foundational skills for all school subjects and life pursuits. Of course there are many mindfulness curricula that can be integrated into schools, but it is important not to reduce mindfulness to a set of exercises. It is a larger philosophy and orientation toward being present in the world.

MINDFULNESS WITHOUT THE MINDFULNESS

We don't need to use the word *mindfulness* if we are bringing this work into schools. This is not some type of deception. *Mindfulness* is a word used for the cultivation of focus and compassion, so if we want to call it focus and compassion training, that is just as well. Some alternative ways to talk about mindfulness are presence, awareness, compassion, empathy, well-being, or self-care. Remember that the greatest goal of mindfulness is to support the flourishing of the most beautiful aspects of our humanity. Whatever we call that, it is important not to be attached to a name or specific exercises. Many incredibly mindful people have never heard the word *mindfulness*.

WORKING WITH RESISTANCE

Always honor resistance. Often the biggest mindfulness proponents begin as the biggest skeptics. Ask good questions of the resisters. Ask them why they are resistant and what preconceived notions they have. If a colleague says they don't have time for mindfulness, this is a great discussion point for time management and stress reduction. If they say that when they try mindfulness it's too frustrating and annoying, this can be a great opportunity to talk about working with difficult emotions and a distracted mind. Bring inquiry and interest to resistance, rather than anger. Resistance carries important information, and being kind and curious toward it is a great way of modeling mindfulness.

KEEP WITHIN RANGE

When offering these practices to colleagues, make sure to give them in digestible pieces. We don't want to have them silently watch their breath for 30 minutes if they have never done this before. This would probably make many of them feel like mindfulness was boring and frustrating. Start with short, directed practices that they will feel successful with and will enjoy. Even 30 seconds of silence can have a strong impact on people.

INSIGHTS AND RECOMMENDATIONS FROM MINDFUL EDUCATION LEADERS

The following recommendations for integrating mindfulness into schools are from some of the leaders in the mindfulness in education movement. Some school systems represented here have been weaving mindfulness into their classrooms for more than 10 years. With these recommendations, we see diverse ways of bringing mindfulness into schools. We also hear from veteran teachers from preschool through high school and with students with various special needs. This is a small introduction to the vast array of organizations and school districts doing this work around the world.

Holistic Life Foundation

The Holistic Life Foundation is a grassroots movement and nonprofit organization teaching mindfulness in the schools of underserved communities. Ali and Atman Smith and Andres Gonzalez began teaching mindfulness in their hometown schools in Baltimore, Maryland. Now many of the students they originally taught have grown up and become mindfulness teachers themselves, working for Holistic Life Foundation teaching mindfulness to thousands of kids around the city. Andy, Atman, and Andres give some recommendation from their own experience of how to incorporate mindfulness into schools.

> There are always some teachers and administrators who are excited and who immediately see the benefits of the program. These are the

people who eventually become our champions and who help advocate to other members of the staff.

> The main resistance that teachers have at first about the program is being concerned that they will not be capable of completing their curriculum due to the time that is being removed for the mindfulness practices.

> If we could only implement one or two things, they would be a period of practice similar to our mindful moment recordings (where students can just be in the present moment and either be quiet or meditate) and an alternative to a suspension room where the youth can get away from the pressures of a school environment and be mindful.

> We understand that not every scenario is going to be ideal, not every location is going to be engaged, and not every staff member is going to have a complete commitment to our program. But just knowing that we can impact at least one person keeps us going, and practicing nonattachment really helps as well!

> Beyond having a wonderful support system and knowing that this is what we were supposed to do in the world, the data that we received was probably the most helpful factor in getting this initiative off the ground. Testimonials and anecdotal evidence only go so far, and experiencing the practice sometimes doesn't seem to be enough, but the numbers seem to be what really gets everyone excited, especially when trying to integrate programs into schools.

> The main effects that mindfulness has had on our students would be in the area of anger management and impulsivity. Youth are much more prone to take a pause and respond instead of react and use their minds instead of their fists to resolve altercations. Focus, concentration, and fewer ruminating thoughts are other externally discernible effects that mindfulness practices have on our students, as well as them becoming more compassionate and empathetic.

Flourish Foundation

The Flourish Foundation is a social profit dedicated to promoting contemplative practices for the purpose of achieving mental balance and universal compassion in communities. Through educational and outreach programs, they introduce mindfulness to students and teachers to support healthy habits of mind in the Idaho Wood River Valley and beyond. The following are recommendations for integrating mindfulness into schools from Ryan Redman, executive director of the Flourish Foundation.

> Initially, we engaged two fifth-grade classrooms with one mindful awareness class per week. Surprisingly, this offering was very well received and over the last five years it has increased to 38 classrooms and 1,000 students receiving training in contemplative practices on a weekly basis.

> From the beginning both teachers and administrators were very excited about the potential of this program. Given the compelling research in the adult community supporting mindfulness interventions, everyone felt there was nothing to lose in trying to integrate contemplative practices into the daily lives of students.

> When we have met with resistance from parents, we invite them into the classrooms and are careful to never pressure teachers in participating.

> We build trusting relationships with teachers and let them take the lead in creating the scheduling of the program.

> Usually at the onset of every mindful awareness offering, teachers feel limited by the amount of time they can invest in the program. However, throughout the process of practicing with their students, teachers develop a new appreciation of time that values quality over quantity. This shift seems to be nurtured by in-depth sharing from their students, who clearly articulate insights they derive from doing the practices and how they can apply these insights to their experiences throughout the day.

> Many teachers find that contemplative practices support the students' readiness to learn and their willingness to interact more thoughtfully and heartfully with other members of their community. An example of this shift is when we had scheduled a three-month intervention for four classrooms in a public school. After three months, the teachers reevaluated their position in wanting only a brief intervention and as a group they decided to extend the program for the rest of the year.

Talk About Wellness

Talk About Wellness (TAW) is an initiative that deepens the inner lives of school children with mindfulness, art, and nature. TAW has worked with several schools and has focused primarily on a private/public partnership with the South Burlington (Vermont) School District and its impressive mindfulness-based programs. TAW helps school districts to find their way toward more peaceful and conscious learning environments. The following are recommendations for integrating mindfulness into schools from Marilyn Webb Neagley, coeditor (with Aostre N. Johnson) of *Educating from the Heart* and director of Talk About Wellness.

> Begin by teaching mindfulness to teachers, counselors, nurses, and try to include other staff, administrators, and parents.
> Sharing emerging neuroscience research on mindfulness and relating it to the problems schools are challenged by gets the attention of administrators, as well as some teachers and parents.
> Use careful language and avoid religious connotations (prayer beads, singing bowls, phrases such as *Namaste, higher power, God,* etc.).
> Convince teachers that this is not another new curriculum or program but a new way of doing what they already are doing.
> Adapt language and practices to the appropriate age/grade levels.
> Working in the upper levels is much more challenging with changing classrooms, more demanding academic requirements, and more extracurricular commitments.
> Mindfulness for teens has generally been offered through advisories, wellness programs, teen mindfulness clubs (meet in mornings or afternoons), and teen retreats. Sometimes educators of all disciplines will encourage moments of silence and breath work before a test, other competition/performance, or at the beginning of a class.
> It's important to have compelling neuroscience as well as evaluative classroom research.
> Begin with start-up funds if possible, for training and resources.
> It is very helpful to have endorsements from superintendents, principals, and curriculum development coordinators.

> Make the materials as "school ready" and relevant as possible: school climate, improved attention, and so on. Use trained teachers to share classroom applications.

Mindfulness and Social-Emotional Learning Group

The following recommendations are from veteran mindfulness educators who are in an ongoing mindfulness and social-emotional learning training with Linda Lantieri and me. Linda is the director of the Inner Resilience program and author of many books, including *Building Emotional Intelligence*. These are recommendations from teachers and administrators who have been doing this work for many years in diverse school environments on what is important to consider when introducing mindfulness into a school.

> Share how mindfulness has helped you in your own life.
> Lead by example and try to embody the work itself by your interaction with colleagues and children.
> Have respect for where your colleagues are in their lives and for what they're already doing in their work with kids.
> Be grounded and nonreactive in the way you teach and share mindfulness.
> Recognize that to cultivate mindfulness, we need to be dedicated to our inner work; for others to develop, they will need their own personal motivation.
> Reassure the other faculty that the mindfulness programs are here to support their work and not create additional curriculum that might ultimately add to their workload.
> It's helpful to hear from peers who are already teaching mindfulness in the classroom and learning about their personal challenges and successes.
> Practice self-care and help the teachers and schools schedule free time during the day for wellness and rejuvenation.
> Find a way to help teachers understand that mindfulness actually helps them find more time in their busy days rather than add another stress.

> It's important to find a community of like-minded peers and a mindfulness buddy to check in with about personal practice as well as the work with kids.

> Be flexible, let go of expectations, and be willing to have fun.

> Be invitational, nonjudgmental, and remember there is no right or wrong answer in mindfulness.

MAKING THE CASE
FOR MINDFULNESS
WORKSHEET

Very often teachers ask me after trainings how they can present mindfulness to their schools or communities so they will be interested in mindfulness. It's good to start small and slow. Begin by simply practicing mindfulness within our schools and communities. Once we feel strong in our own practices, there are many great benefits we can share. The research and experiential benefits of mindfulness are important selling points. Below is a worksheet to use whenever we are thinking of presenting mindfulness to an administration or larger audience.

MAKING THE CASE FOR MINDFULNESS

Motivation: What is your motivation for giving this presentation? What effect do you hope to have?

_____

_____

_____

Core Message: What is the core message you want your audience to leave with?

_____

_____

_____

Audience Experience: How would you like your audience to feel in their minds, hearts, and bodies during and after the talk?

_____

_____

_____

Presence: How do you want to feel as you are giving this talk? What do you need to maintain the presence you hope to convey?

_____

_____

_____

Audience Demographic: Who is your audience? What is the demographic of the participants, what are their roles in education, and how familiar might they be with mindfulness?

_____

_____

_____

Selling Points: What are the selling points for this group? Are they looking for validated research on mindfulness? Do they want personal tools for relaxation?

_____

_____

_____

Possible Resistance: What are some possible sensitivities in this group? How can you be cognizant of your language so you meet minimal resistance?

_____

_____

_____

What's the Problem?: Choose one or two problems that your audience will relate to in their own lives and they see their students facing for which mindfulness can be an antidote.

_____

_____

_____

Learning Objectives: Choose learning objectives to focus on that are developed with mindfulness and are directly correlated to relieving the problems from the previous question.

_____

_____

_____

Leading a Practice: Think of some experiential mindfulness practices to lead your audience in that use mindfulness to develop the chosen learning objectives.

_____

_____

_____

Power of Storytelling: Think of a story that elucidates the way mindfulness can work with the problem you have chosen and how the practices develop the learning objectives.

_____

_____

_____

Mindful Science: Find some researched benefits of mindfulness for adults and youth that reflect the learning objectives you will be focusing on.

_____

_____

_____

Mindful Opening and Closing: Think of a mindfulness-based ritual to open and close the sessions. It could simply be the ring of a bell, taking several breaths together, or you could send good wishes to the students you are providing for.

_____

_____

_____

Process Reflection: How do you feel in your body, mind, and heart about giving this presentation. What else might you need before you are ready?

_____

_____

_____

SUMMING UP

Now that we have come to the conclusion of this workbook, the philosophy and practices are ours to take and explore and share with our communities. The way each person practices mindfulness will look different. Maybe our practice is that immediately after waking we remember to be kind to ourselves and greet the sun with appreciation for another day to be alive. Or our practice could be mindfully exercising and stretching our bodies, noticing the intricate sensations and harmonizing the breath to the movements. A mindfulness practice is an utterly personal thing. It's the unique way we connect with ourselves, reverently becoming our own best friends. Mindfulness becomes our ally. When we are stressed, mindfulness is only one breath away.

We can be as creative as possible with mindfulness when bringing it into our schools. Maybe we bring in some organic and conventional strawberries and lead a mindful eating practice to allow students to find the difference in tastes. Or we could play some nice rhythms and have kids play flow and tell, rapping in a circle about what's happening in the present moment. The secret to making any lesson into a mindfulness practice is having the students pause and notice what's happening inside. During lunch or on the playground, we can instruct students to pause and notice what's happening inside and all around them when we ring a bell.

We all find our own style of teaching mindfulness. Remember to incorporate the physical, mental, emotional, social, and global literacies. Be careful not to simply use mindfulness as a mental focusing practice. Though focusing is an important skill on its own, to make it mindfulness, we want students to be relaxed in their bodies, open their hearts, and be conscious of their relationships to the social and global realms. When we gain all five literacies and teach them to our students, we are supporting integrity, responsibility, and wisdom.

Kindergarten teachers usually remember this, but in older grades we can forget that a major part of our jobs is to steer students toward becoming healthy and honorable human beings. With mindfulness we can help them build the attributes they need to thrive and make a positive impact in the world. When students are relaxed, attentive, and socially literate, they are more ready to learn and succeed. Teaching mindfulness to our students makes our job easier and more fulfilling when we see our students growing.

Research has shown that learning improves and school conflicts fall when mindfulness is part of a school. We see something even more profound—kids strengthening capacities for regulation, happiness, and compassion, which they will be able to use their entire lives. The healing of our society requires more people who can empathize, being attuned to the needs of others. The healing of our natural environment requires people who are attuned to the needs of the planet. We teach mindfulness with the hope that each individual will find peace themselves. Then we hope this inner peace can create outer peace around the world.

References

Biegel, G. M., Brown, K. W., Shapiro, S. L., & Schubert, C. M. (2009). Mindfulness-based stress reduction for the treatment of adolescent psychiatric outpatients: A randomized clinical trial. *Journal of Consulting and Clinical Psychology*, 77, 855–866.

Brefczynski-Lewis, J. A., Lutz, A., Schaefer, H. S., Levinson, D. B., & Davidson, R. J. (2007). Neural correlates of attentional expertise in long-term meditation practitioners. *Proceedings of the National Academy of Sciences USA*, 104, 11483–11488.

Broderick, P. C., & Metz, S. (2009). Learning to BREATHE: a pilot trial of a mindfulness curriculum for adolescents. *Advances in School Mental Health Promotion*, 2(1), 35–46.

Colzato, L. S., Ozturk, A., and Hommel, B. (2012). Meditate to create: the impact of focused-attention and open-monitoring training on convergent and divergent thinking. *Frontiers in Psychology*, 3, 116, doi: 10.3389/fpsyg.2012.00116.

Efklides, A. (2011). Interactions of metacognition with motivation and affect in self-regulated learning: the MASRL model. *Educational Psychologist*, 46(1), 6–25.

Felitti, V. J., Anda, R.F., Nordenberg, D., Williamson, D. F., Spitz, A.M., Edwards, V., Koss, M.P., et al. (1998). The relationship of adult health status to childhood abuse and household dysfunction. *American Journal of Preventive Medicine*, 14, 245–258.

Flook, L., Goldberg, S. B., Pinger, L., & Davidson, R. J. (2015). Promoting prosocial behavior and self-regulatory skills in preschool children through a mindfulness-based kindness curriculum. *Developmental Psychology*, 51(1), 44–51.

Flook, L., Smalley, S. L., Kitil, M. J., Galla, B., Kaiser-Greenland, S., Locke, J., Ishijima, E., & Kasari, C. (2010). Effects of mindful awareness practices on executive functions in elementary school children. *Journal of Applied School Psychology*, 26, 70–95.

Goff, P. A., Jackson, M. C., Di Leone, B. A. L., Culotta, C. M., & DiTomasso, N. A. (2014). The essence of innocence: consequences of dehumanizing black children. *Journal of Personality and Social Psychology*, 106(4), 526–545.

Greenberg, J., Reiner, K., & Meiran, N. (2012). "Mind the trap": mindfulness practice reduces cognitive rigidity. *PLoS One*, 7:e36206, doi: 10.1371/journal.pone.0036206.

Hanson, J. L., Chung, M. K., Avants, B. B., Shritcliff, E. A., Gee, J. C., Davidson, R. J., & Pollak, S. D. (2010). Early stress is associated with alterations in the orbitofrontal cortex: a tensor-based morphometry investigation of brain structure and behavioral risk. *Journal of Neuroscience*, 30(22), 7466–7472.

Hölzel, B. K., et al. (2011). Mindfulness practice leads to increases in regional brain grey matter density. *Psychiatry Resesarch*, 191, 36–43.

Jennings, P. A. (2015). *Mindfulness for teachers: Simple skills for peace and productivity in the classroom* (The Norton Series on the Social Neuroscience of Education). New York: W. W. Norton.

Jennings, P. A., Brown, J. L., Frank, J. L., Doyle, S., Oh, Y., Tanler, R., Rasheed, D., DeWeese, A., DeMauro, A. A. & Greenberg, M. T. (2016, April). Enhancing teachers' wellbeing and classroom quality: Results from a randomized controlled trail of CARE. In P. Jennings (Chair). *Examining Implementation, Process, and Outcomes of CARE for Teachers, a Mindfulness-based Intervention*. Symposium presented at the American Education Research Association Annual Conference, Washington, D. C.

Kang, Y., Gray, J. R., & Dovidio, J.F. (2014). The nondiscriminating heart: lovingkindness meditation training decreases implicit intergroup bias. *Journal of Experimental Psychology: General*, 143(3), 1306–1313, doi: 10.1037/a0034150.

Killingsworth, M. A., & Gilbert, D. T. (2010). A wandering mind is an unhappy mind. Science, 330(6006), 932, doi: 10.1126/science.1192439.

Leung, A. K., Kim, S., Polman, E., Ong, L., Qiu, L., Goncalo, J. A., & San-chez-Burks, J. (2011). Embodied metaphors and creative "acts." [Electronic version]. Retrieved December 15, 2015, from Cornell University, ILR School, http://digitalcommons.ilr.cornell.edu/articles/486/.

Lueke, A., & Gibson, B. (2014). Mindfulness meditation reduces implicit age and race bias: the role of reduced automaticity of responding. *Social Psychological and Personality Science*, 2014, 1–8.

Lutz, A., Brefczynski-Lewis, J. A., Johnstone, T., & Davidson, R. J. (2008). Regulation of the neural circuitry of emotion by compassion meditation: effects of meditative expertise. *PLoS One*, 3(3), e1897.

Lutz, J., et al. (2014). Mindfulness and emotion regulation—an fMRI study. *Social Cognitive and Affective Neuroscience*, 9, 776–785.

Metz, S. M., Frank, J. L., Riebel, D., Cantrell, T., Sanders, R., & Broderick, P. C. (2013) The effectiveness of the Learning to BREATHE program on adolescent emotion regulation. *Research in Human Development*, 10(3), 252–272, doi: 10.1080/15427609.2013.818488.

Moore, A., & Malinowski, P. (2009). Meditation, mindfulness and cognitive flexibility. *Consciousness and Cognition*, 18, 176–186, doi: 10.1016/j.concog.2008.12.008.

Neff, K. D., & McGehee, P. (2010). Self-compassion and psychological resilience among adolescents and young adults. *Self and Identity*, 9(3), 225–240.

Perikkou, A., Gavrieli, A., Kougioufa, M. M., Tzirkali, M., & Yannakoulia, M. (2013). A novel approach for increasing fruit consumption in children. *Journal of the Academy of Nutrition Dietetics*, 113(9), 1188–1193, doi: 10.1016/j.jand.2013.05.024.

Roeser, R. W., Schonert-Reichl, K. A., Jha, A., Cullen, M., Wallace, L., Wilensky, R., Oberle, E., Thomson, K., Taylor, C., & Harrison, J. (2013). Mindfulness training and reductions in teacher stress and burnout: results from two randomized, waitlist-control field trials. *Journal of Educational Psychology*, 105(3), 787–804, doi: 10.1037/a0032093.

Schonert-Reichl, K. A., Oberle, E., Lawlor, M. S., Abbott, D., Thomson, K., Oberlander, T. F., & Diamond, A. (2015). Enhancing cognitive and social-emotional development through a simple-to-administer mindfulness-based school program for elementary school children: a randomized controlled trial. *Developmental Psychology*, 51(1), 52-66.

Semple, R. J., Lee, J., Rosa, D., & Miller, L. F. (2010). A randomized trial of mindfulness-based cognitive therapy for children: promoting mindful attention to enhance social-emotional resiliency in children. *Journal of Child and Family Studies*, 19(2), 218–229.

Singh, N., et al. (2007). Adolescents with conduct disorder can be mindful of their aggressive behavior. *Journal of Emotional and Behavioral Disorders*, 15(1), 56–63.

Tang, Y.-Y., Hölzel, B. K., & Posner, M. I. (2015). The neuroscience of mindfulness meditation. *Nature Reviews Neuroscience*, 16, 213–225.

Tang, Y. Y., Yang, L., Leve, L. D., & Harold, G. T. (2012). Improving executive function and its neurobiological mechanisms through a mindfulness-based intervention: advances within the field of developmental neuroscience. *Child Development Perspectives*, 6, 361–366.

Teasdale, J.D. (1999). Metacognition, mindfulness and the modification of mood disorders. *Clinical Psychology and Psychotherapy*, 6(2), 146-155.

U.S. Department of Education Office for Civil Rights. (2014). 23 Civil Rights Data Collection: Data Snapshot (School Discipline).

Vestergaard-Poulsen, P., et al. (2009). Long-term meditation is associated with increased grey matter density in the brain stem. *Neuroreport*, 20, 170–174.

Zenner, C., Herrnleben-Kurz, S., & Walach, H. (2014). Mindfulness-based interventions in schools—a systematic review and meta-analysis. *Frontiers in Psychology*, 5, 603.

Zoogman, S., Goldberg, S. B., Hoyt, W. T., & Miller, L. (2014). Mindfulness interventions with youth: a meta-analysis. *Mindfulness*, 6(2), 290–302.

Index

integration, 211–20 (*see also specific practices and* integration practices)

mindful life (*see* mindful life practice)

mindfulness, 66–76 (*see also* mindfulness practice(s))

projection
    awareness of, 43
    introspection and, 43

quality(ies)
    positive, 167–70 (*see also* positive qualities lesson)

question(s)
    dialogue (*see specific types and lessons, e.g.,* playing mindfulness lesson)

questioning assumptions, 77–80
    carrying about inequality in, 78–79
    discernment in, 79
    know we don't know in, 79
    learning about our world in, 79
    lesson on, 184–87 (*see also* questioning assumptions lesson)
    method of, 78–80
    mindfulness in, 77–80
    noting emotions in, 79
    thought spotting in, 79
    turning inward in, 79

questioning assumptions lesson, 184–87
    age and stage, 186–87
    described, 185
    dialogue questions, 186
    inspiring quote, 186
    journaling prompts, 186

learning objectives, 184
mindful life practice, 186
preparation and considerations, 184

range of group
    learning, 57–58

reactivity
    in engaging your audience in mindfulness, 61

Rechtschaffen, D., 39, 243

recommendation(s)
    integration, 221–49 (*see also specific types and* integration recommendations)

recording(s)
    in mindfulness in education, 2–3

reflection
    mindful, 108–10

regulation
    emotional, 226

relaxation
    deep, 122–24, 227 (*see also* deep relaxation lesson)
    defined, 227
    in physical literacy, 17–18

reminder(s)
    mindful, 224

reporting back
    in mindfulness lesson, 99

resilience
    defined, 96
    as mindful learning objective, 96–97

resistance
    working with, 238

Roosevelt, E., 153

roots of emotions lesson, 155–58
    age and stage, 157–58
    described, 156